English Practice Papers

Level 5
English

For information regarding permission, write to:
Scholastic Education International (Singapore) Private Limited
81 Ubi Avenue 4, #02-28 UB.ONE, Singapore 408830
Email: education@scholastic.com.sg

For sales enquiries, write to:

India
Scholastic India Pvt. Ltd.
A-27, Ground Floor, Bharti Sigma Centre
Infocity-1, Sector 34, Gurgaon (Haryana) - 122001
Email: education@scholastic.co.in

Rest of the World
Scholastic Education International (Singapore) Pte Ltd
81 Ubi Avenue 4, #02-28 UB.ONE, Singapore 408830
Email: education@scholastic.com.sg

Visit our website: www.scholastic.com.sg

First edition 2014

ISBN 978-981-07-7572-8

Welcome to studySMART !

SCHOLASTIC

English Practice Papers provides opportunities for the systematic assessment of the important components of language acquisition – vocabulary, grammar and reading comprehension.

Assessment is important for consolidating knowledge and skills, allowing you and your child to monitor progress and identify areas of strength and weakness.

Each practice paper is designed to cover various aspects of questions that your child may encounter in English tests. In each practice paper, your child will complete a wide range of exercises that test his reading and editing skills, and vocabulary and grammar.

How to use this book?

1. Set aside a quiet and clutter-free place for your child to complete the practice paper. Set a time limit if you like to help him manage his time during an actual test.

2. Introduce the target skill at the beginning of each section and direct his attention to the number of marks allocated for each answer.

3. Let your child complete the entire practice paper.

4. Check the answers and record the marks for each section and the total for the practice paper in the Marking Scheme at the beginning of the book.

5. As your child completes more practice papers, you will be able to chart their progress and identify strengths and weaknesses in the Marking Scheme table.

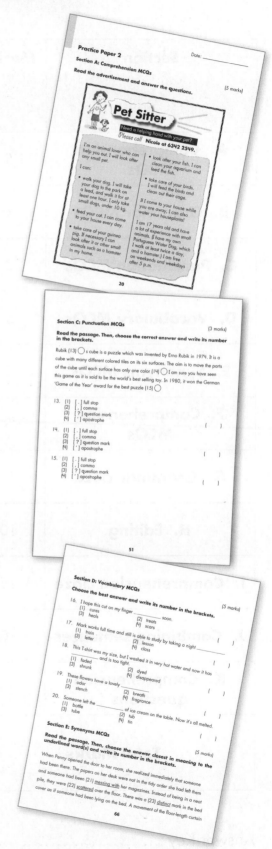

Contents and Marking Scheme

Section	Marks	Practice Paper 1 p. 6 Date:	Practice Paper 2 p. 20	Practice Pap p. 34
A. Comprehension MCQs	5			
B. Grammar MCQs	7			
C. Punctuation MCQs	3			
D. Vocabulary MCQs	5			
E. Synonyms MCQs	5			
F. Comprehension MCQs	5			
G. Grammar cloze	10			
H. Editing	10			
I. Comprehension cloze	15			
J. Combining sentences	10			
K. Comprehension questions	20			
Total Marks		95	95	

ctice Paper 4 p. 48	Practice Paper 5 p. 62	Practice Paper 6 p. 78	Practice Paper 7 p. 94	Practice Paper 8 p. 109
95	95	95	95	95

Practice Paper I

Section A: Comprehension MCQs   (5 marks)

Read the advertisement and answer the questions.

A cool place to stay?

Don't delay. Book today!

The Ice Hotel in Norland, Sweden, is a truly original place. Built out of ice and snow every November, it disappears every spring as it melts. Sculpted by world-famous designers, the hotel changes its architecture every year.

This unusual hotel has more than 80 rooms and offers a wide range of outdoor activities including:

- Snowmobile safaris
- Cross-country skiing
- Fishing in frozen lakes
- Helicopter tours

After an exciting day, relax in the sauna before watching a movie in the hotel's cinema.

Delicious gourmet meals are served in the restaurant and guests can enjoy a cold drink at the bar in a glass carved from ice.

Although the inside temperature is around −5°C, the outside temperature can drop to as low as −40°C, so bring warm clothing. You won't feel the cold though, when you crawl into your high-tech thermal sleeping bag on your ice-block bed. The 'beds' are covered with reindeer hides to ensure a warm night's sleep.

Call our reservations department:
+46 (0) 980 66800 or email: info@icehotel.com

Choose the correct answer and write its number in the brackets.

1. The Ice Hotel is rebuilt every year _____.
   (1) to change its architecture each year
   (2) because it is in Sweden
   (3) because every spring it melts and disappears
   (4) to make it a truly original place   (3)

2. Which of the following activities is not available?
   (1) a tour in a helicopter
   (2) downhill skiing
   (3) fishing
   (4) sauna   (4)

3. Cold drinks are served at the bar because _____.
   (1) no one drinks hot drinks
   (2) it is too hot to drink anything but a cold drink
   (3) a hot drink would melt the 'glass' made of ice
   (4) it is −5°C   (3)

4. The outdoor temperature _____.
   (1) is always below −40°C
   (2) is around −5°C
   (3) is above −40°C
   (4) can fall to −40°C   (4)

5. You won't feel cold in bed because _____.
   (1) the bedrooms are centrally-heated
   (2) the bedrooms are not in the Ice Hotel
   (3) there are special bed sheets and blankets
   (4) you will need to bring the correct warm clothes   (3)

Section B: Grammar MCQs   (7 marks)

Choose the correct answer and write its number in the brackets.

6. If Harry invites me to his party, I _____ him to mine.
    (1) invite   (2) inviting
    (3) will invite   (4) invites   (3)

7. You should go to the library before 10 o'clock. There are _____ people then.
    (1) the few   (2) more few
    (3) fewest   (4) fewer   (4)

8. Start to tidy up now. The bell _____ in 5 minutes.
    (1) going   (2) will go
    (3) go   (4) is to go   (2)

9. What shall we do this afternoon?
    I don't mind. _____ you like.
    (1) Nothing   (2) Everything
    (3) Anyone   (4) Anything   (4)

10. When Jerry arrived, it _____ with rain.
    (1) was pouring   (2) has pouring
    (3) will pour   (4) pours   (1)

11. Mr Jay doesn't think we _____ the inter-school competition.
    (1) shall enter   (2) ought enter
    (3) have enter   (4) should enter   (1)

12. By the time Ken reached the bus stop, the bus _____.
    (1) has already left   (2) had already left
    (3) had already leave   (4) had already leaving   (2)

Section C: Punctuation MCQs   (3 marks)

Read the passage. Then, choose the correct answer and write its number in the brackets.

"Excuse me, Madam. Could I ask you a few questions (13) ◯

"Well, as long as it doesn't take too long. I'm waiting for my bus. It should be here soon."

"Just ten short questions about your shopping habits. Do you do all your shopping here?"

"No, just for my children (14) ◯ s clothes."

"Could you tell me why?"

"No, I'm sorry I can't. Here's my bus (15) ◯

13. (1) [."] full stop and quotation marks
    (2) [,"] comma and quotation marks
    (3) [?"] question mark and quotation marks
    (4) ["?] quotation marks and question mark   (3)

14. (1) [.] full stop
    (2) [,] comma
    (3) ['] apostrophe
    (4) [?] question mark   (3)

15. (1) [!"] exclamation mark and quotation marks
    (2) [!] exclamation mark
    (3) ["] quotation marks
    (4) [.] full stop   (1)

9

Section D: Vocabulary MCQs   (5 marks)

Choose the best answer and write its number in the brackets.

16. Mark arrived late for work today due to the _____ traffic on
    the roads.
    (1) strong   (2) great
    (3) heavy   (4) big   (3)

17. The police took _____ of all the suspects.
    (1) fingerprints   (2) fingermarks
    (3) fingers   (4) tracks   (1)

18. When Marie let the dog off the lead, it _____ and she never
    saw it again.
    (1) ran up   (2) ran in
    (3) ran on   (4) ran off   (4)

19. This orange juice is past its _____ date.
    (1) sell-by   (2) sell-after
    (3) sale   (4) sell-for   (1)

20. I need to _____ an important call. Can I use your phone?
    (1) do   (2) make
    (3) have   (4) try   (2)

Section E: Synonyms MCQs   (5 marks)

**Read the passage. Then, choose the answer closest in meaning to the
underlined word(s) and write its number in the brackets.**

George woke up in the night with a (21) raging thirst. He got out of bed and

(22) crept downstairs, trying to make as little noise as possible. Slowly turning the

kitchen door knob, he pushed open the door. He reached up to the cupboard, took out a glass and filled it to the (23) <u>brim</u> with cold water. As he drank it he wondered what had (24) <u>provoked</u> this unusual thirst. Then he remembered the two packets of potato chips he had (25) <u>gorged on</u> when he had come home that evening.

21. (1) slight   (2) painful
     (3) annoying   (4) strong   (4)

22. (1) moved quietly   (2) ran
     (3) fell   (4) jumped   (1)

23. (1) halfway mark   (2) top
     (3) bottom   (4) middle   (2)

24. (1) quenched   (2) done
     (3) caused   (4) stopped   (3)

25. (1) bought   (2) greedily eaten
     (3) made   (4) opened   (2)

Section F: Comprehension MCQs   (5 marks)

Read the passage and answer the questions.

Scientists have discovered a fungus that can withstand high levels of radiation. Inside the highly radioactive Chernobyl nuclear power station, a black fungus was found to be growing.

The nuclear reactor in the Chernobyl power station exploded over 20 years ago, releasing huge amounts of harmful radiation into the surrounding area. Many people were killed and the reactor itself is still highly dangerous. The town was evacuated and the nuclear power station was sealed off. Since the explosion,

5

scientists have been carrying out studies into the causes of the accident and the effects on the environment.

Due to the high amounts of radiation still present in the power station, no person **10** can enter the compound, but robots can be used to carry out experiments. Scientists sent a robot to take samples of a black substance seen on the inside walls of the reactor. When this substance was examined, to the scientists' surprise, it was discovered to be a living organism — a fungus.

The scientists were amazed to find a living organism in such an environment. **15** This special fungus contains a substance called melanin which enables it to use the radioactivity as a source of energy. The melanin in the fungus acts like chlorophyll in green plants, **harnessing** energy.

What is the significance of this discovery? It does not mean that the fungi can make the radioactive material harmless again, but the fungi can grow in an **20** environment that is harmful to every other form of life. The fungi could be used as a food source on trips into space. On long space voyages, storing enough food for the astronauts is always a problem. It is possible that these fungi, or different versions of them, could use the radioactivity in space as a source of energy. In turn, the fungi could be a food source for the space crew. **25**

Choose the correct answer and write its number in the brackets.

26. The town near the Chernobyl power station was evacuated because
_____.
    (1) a black substance was found in the reactor
    (2) scientists wanted to carry out experiments
    (3) the power station had exploded, releasing
    radiation into the area
    (4) a fungus had been found   (3)

27. Why were robots used to do the experiments?
    (1) Robots were less expensive than people.
    (2) The nuclear power station was too dangerous for people to go into.
    (3) The fungi were harmful to people.
    (4) The robots were already in the reactor.   (2)

28. The scientists were surprised to find a fungus growing inside the reactor
    because _____.
    (1) it contained melanin
    (2) Chernobyl exploded over 20 years ago
    (3) a robot was used for the experiment
    (4) the levels of radiation were extremely high   (4)

29. The word 'harnessing' in line 18 means _____.
    (1) trapping and using
    (2) pulling
    (3) injuring
    (4) giving out   (1)

30. The fungi could _____.
    (1) be used as a source of food for astronauts
    (2) make radioactive places safe again
    (3) be radioactive
    (4) protect people from too much sunlight   (1)

13

Section G: Grammar cloze   (10 marks)

Choose the correct word(s) from the box for each blank. Write its letter in the blank. Use each word(s) once.

A	more	B	on	C	than	D	as
E	in	F	at	G	to	H	of
J	in order to	K	these	L	from	M	as a result
N	that	P	although	Q	instead of		

Cooking programs (31) ____B____ television are extremely popular in Britain. These programs feature celebrity chefs showing how (32) ____G____ make delicious meals. So, you would think that people watch these programs (33) ____J____ learn how to cook and to discover new recipes. (34) ____M____ you would imagine that people in Britain must love cooking and enjoy eating meals (35) ____F____ home. In fact, a recent survey has shown that more British adults are turning to easy-to-prepare ready meals (36) ____C____ ever before. The country is the biggest consumer (37) ____H____ microwave meals in Europe. Nearly one in four British adults eat ready meals (38) ____A____ than once a week. Manufacturers of ready meals have responded to this increase (39) ____E____ demand, and have adapted their products to the market. They have developed a greater range of meals and, (40) ____P____ the meals are still factory-made, they contain more organic and natural products.

Section H: Editing (10 marks)

The words in bold have spelling errors and the underlined words are grammatical errors. Write the correct word(s) in the box.

(41) _____ (42) _____

A boy's bicycle was **stollen** yesterday from the bike rack outside the **swiming** pool.

(43) _____

Peter Hawkins had <u>leaved</u> his bike in the rack while he went for his swimming lesson.

(44) _____

As Peter returned to the bike rack with his friends he **imediately** noticed that his

(45) _____ (46) _____

bike was missing. "I'm pretty sure I <u>lock</u> my bike," said a **distraut** Peter. "I hope

(47) _____

that whoever took it, <u>bring</u> it back. I had just oiled it and pumped up the tires. It was

(48) _____

working <u>beautiful</u>." If you were near the area yesterday and saw anything

(49) _____ (50) _____

suspisious, please contact your <u>near</u> police station.

Section I: Comprehension cloze (15 marks)

Read and fill in each blank with the best word.

A television timeout is a short break in a sporting event to allow advertisements to

(51) _____ shown. This commercial break occurs during a period when

the game has (52) _____ stopped. For example in soccer, during the

halftime break, advertisements (53) _____ shown. In tennis, between

15

every odd-numbered game (54) _____ the players change ends, they take a short break. There is (55) _____ time to show a quick advert.

Of course, companies want to advertize their products when (56) _____ highest number of people will be watching. They want to reach the biggest audience they (57) _____. An important soccer match, for example, will attract thousands (58) _____ viewers. Since this is a peak program, in terms of popularity, (59) _____ a company advertizes during such a match, it will cost more (60) _____ than during a less popular program. During the Olympic Games, or Soccer World Cup, hundreds of thousands of dollars are (61) _____ from advertizing alone.

For the television (62) _____, these timeouts, or commercial breaks, can be an opportunity to take a short (63) _____ from watching television. They can grab a drink or snack or (64) _____ to the toilet. Naturally, the companies advertizing their (65) _____ hope they sit and watch the ads.

Section J: Combining sentences   (10 marks)

Rewrite the sentence(s) using the words given. Your answer must be in one sentence and its meaning must be the same as that of the given sentence(s).

66.   A decorator is painting our living room.

      Our living room _____

      _____

67.   Caroline moved to Brazil in 2006. She is still living here.

      _____ lived _____ since

      _____

16

68. "Would you like something to drink?" asked my mother.

My mother asked _____

_____

69. The tennis match was canceled because it was raining.

_____ because of

_____

70. Penny was very hungry when she got home from school. She ate a whole packet of cookies.

_____ so _____

that _____

Section K: Comprehension questions   (20 marks)

Read the passage and answer the questions. Write your answers in complete sentences.

What is the most dangerous animal on Earth? It is rarely longer than 16 mm and

weighs about 2.5 g. It can travel at 1–2 km/hour and fly for up to 4 hours.

It is nocturnal, spending most of the day resting in a cool place. Have you guessed

what it is? The mosquito!

Mosquitos spread serious diseases such as malaria, which causes the deaths of   **5**

5 million people a year. The female mosquito sucks blood from humans and other

animals, as part of its feeding habits. If it sucks blood from a person infected with

a disease, the blood will contain viruses or other germs. The next person the

mosquito bites can be infected with this disease. A virus can be spread through

the mosquito's saliva into the blood of the next person.   **10**

In many areas of the world mosquitos just cause unpleasant itchy bites. But in other parts, such as Africa and South America, they spread malaria and yellow fever as well as other life-threatening illnesses.

Man has fought against the mosquito in various ways. One way is to destroy their breeding ground. Mosquitos require water to reproduce, so by keeping the   **15** land dry, mosquitos cannot multiply. Another way is to prevent the mosquitos from biting humans. This can be done with insect repellent, a chemical substance that you rub onto your skin. **This** keeps the insects away. Sleeping under mosquito nets at night also stops the insects biting. Scientists are also trying to develop vaccines that would provide immunity to diseases that are transmitted by the insect.   **20** Hopefully one day we will win the fight against the most dangerous animal on Earth.

71.   How big is a mosquito?

_____

_____

72.   Which word in paragraph 1 means something sleeps in the day and is active at night?

_____

_____

73.   Why is the mosquito described as the most dangerous animal on Earth?

_____

_____

_____

74. How does a mosquito pass a disease from one person to another?

_____

_____

75. What two examples of diseases spread by mosquitos are given?

_____

_____

76. How can keeping the land dry stop mosquitos from breeding?

_____

_____

77. What does 'this' refer to in line 18?

_____

_____

78. Why do people sleep under nets?

_____

_____

79. What do vaccines do?

_____

_____

80. Do you agree that mosquitos are the most dangerous animals on Earth?

_____

_____

Date: _30/11/15_

Practice Paper 2

Section A: Comprehension MCQs   (5 marks)

Read the advertisement and answer the questions.

Pet Sitter

Need a helping hand with your pet?

Please call **Nicole at 6342 2549.**

I'm an animal lover who can help you out. I will look after any small pet.

I can:

- walk your dog. I will take your dog to the park on a lead, and walk it for at least one hour. I only take small dogs, under 10 kg.

- feed your cat. I can come to your house every day.

- take care of your guinea pig. If necessary I can look after it or other small animals such as a hamster in my home.

- look after your fish. I can clean your aquarium and feed the fish.

- take care of your birds. I will feed the birds and clean out their cage.

If I come to your house while you are away, I can also water your houseplants!

I am 17 years old and have a lot of experience with small animals. (I have my own Portuguese Water Dog, which I walk at least twice a day, and a hamster.) I am free on weekends and weekdays after 5 p.m.

20

Choose the correct answer and write its number in the brackets.

1. The pet sitter will not look after _____.
    - (1) any small pet
    - (3) guinea pigs
    - (3) dogs over 10 kg
    - (4) fish   ( )

2. The pet sitter will take into her own home _____.
    - (1) guinea pigs only
    - (2) small animals
    - (3) any cat
    - (4) big dogs only   ( )

3. The pet sitter will _____.
    - (1) feed your cat
    - (2) let the birds fly around the room
    - (3) clean fish ponds
    - (4) walk your dog for at least 2 hours   ( )

4. The pet sitter has her own _____.
    - (1) hamster and dog
    - (2) dog and guinea pig
    - (3) cat and fish
    - (4) hamster and fish   ( )

5. The pet sitter is only free on _____.
    - (1) weekday evenings
    - (2) weekends
    - (3) Saturdays
    - (4) weekday evenings and weekends   ( )

Section B: Grammar MCQs   (7 marks)

Choose the correct answer and write its number in the brackets.

6. Many tourists enjoy _____ Singapore's open-air hawker centers for local food.
   (1) to visit   (2) visit
   (3) visited   (4) visiting   (   )

7. That blue pen on the desk is _____.
   (1) Mary's   (2) Marys
   (3) Marys'   (4) Mary   (   )

8. Ken _____ come with us, so let's not wait for him.
   (1) should not   (2) might not
   (3) must   (4) shall not   (   )

9. I'm sorry, I've picked up the wrong bag. This one is not _____.
   (1) mine   (2) my
   (3) our   (4) me   (   )

10. There's no need to shout _____ me.
    (1) with   (2) by
    (3) of   (4) at   (   )

11. Miss Lee _____ at this school since 2001.
    (1) is teaching   (2) teaches
    (3) has taught   (4) taught   (   )

12. Mark went for a _____ this morning.
    (1) three-miles run   (2) three-mile run
    (3) run three miles   (4) three-mile runs   (   )

22

Section C: Punctuation MCQs   (3 marks)

Read the passage. Then, choose the correct answer and write its number in the brackets.

My aunt Sally (13) ◯ who lives in Canada, phones me every year on my

birthday. Last year she told me about the very cold winters they have there, "It's so

cold (14) ◯ she said, "that we can't stay outside for more than 10 minutes (15) ◯ "

I can't imagine living in a country where it's cold. Here, where I live, it's always

warm, even when it's raining!

13.   (1)   [.] full stop
      (2)   [,] comma
      (3)   [?] question mark
      (4)   ['] apostrophe   (   )

14.   (1)   [."] full stop and quotation marks
      (2)   [,"] comma and quotation marks
      (3)   ["] quotation marks
      (4)   [,] comma   (   )

15.   (1)   [!] exclamation mark
      (2)   [,] comma
      (3)   [?] question mark
      (4)   ['] apostrophe   (   )

Section D: Vocabulary MCQs   (5 marks)

Choose the best answer and write its number in the brackets.

16. They are digging a hole in the road because a water pipe has _____.
    (1)   bust   (2) broke
    (3)   frozen   (4) burst   (   )

17. Would you like me to give you _____ with the chores?
    (1)   a hand   (2) a finger
    (3)   a help   (4) an arm   (   )

18. Mr and Mrs Cuff _____ an apartment for a week in Florida.
    (1)   hired   (2) stayed
    (3)   lodged   (4) rented   (   )

19. Water is the best thing to _____ a thirst.
    (1)   stop   (2) beat
    (3)   quench   (4) halt   (   )

20. The horse _____ its ears when the rider came into the stable.
    (1)   turned up   (2) pricked up
    (3)   stood up   (4) put up   (   )

Section E: Synonyms MCQs   (5 marks)

Read the passage. Then, choose the answer closest in meaning to the underlined word(s) and write its number in the brackets.

Waiting outside the principal's office, Joy's heart was (21) <u>thumping</u> in her chest. She had been (22) <u>summoned</u> to see the principal at 10 o'clock and now she was nervously waiting until (23) <u>the dot of</u> 10 before she knocked on the door. What had she done? Why did the principal want to see her? Suddenly the door opened and

Lee from Grade 5 came out. His eyes were (24) <u>brimming with</u> tears. But before Joy could speak to him and ask him what was wrong, a (25) <u>stern</u> voice called her into the office.

21.　(1)　hurting　　　　　　　(2)　banging
　　　(3)　beating　　　　　　　(4)　knocking　　　　　　　　　(2)

22.　(1)　ordered　　　　　　　(2)　asked
　　　(3)　said　　　　　　　　(4)　thought　　　　　　　　　(1)

23.　(1)　almost　　　　　　　(2)　after
　　　(3)　before　　　　　　　(4)　exactly　　　　　　　　　(4)

24.　(1)　dry of　　　　　　　(2)　full of
　　　(3)　empty of　　　　　　(4)　salty with　　　　　　　　(2)

25.　(1)　friendly　　　　　　(2)　serious
　　　(3)　quiet　　　　　　　(4)　loud　　　　　　　　　　(2)

Section F: Comprehension MCQs　　　　　　　　　　(5 marks)

Read the passage and answer the questions.

If you enjoy sports and are looking for a new challenge, why not try a triathlon? This sport involves three different sports: running, swimming and cycling. If you can do all of these things, triathlons could be for you.

Ever since the triathlon became an Olympic sport in Australia in 2000, it has become very popular. The annual triathlon in London attracts over 10,000　　**5** competitors. Of course, you will not be able to enter the London Triathlon straightaway, but with regular training, you can build on your abilities and enjoy yourself at the same time.

One advantage of this sport is that you don't need a lot of equipment. For running, you only need a good pair of shoes, and for swimming, a swimming costume. **10** For cycling, you do need a bicycle, but for beginners it is not necessary to have a top-of-the-range racing bike. If you are really good at cycling, it is possible to find a sponsor who would pay for a better bike for you.

In a triathlon, the events take place one after the other, without a break. Swimming is usually first, followed by cycling and then running. The junior events **15** involve a 100 m swim, a 5 km cycle, and a 1 km run. These distances are increased according to the age of the competitors. The beginner distances are a 300 m swim, an 8 km cycle, and a 2 km run. The top adult distances are extremely long and only the fittest can attempt them. The competitors swim for 3.8 km, cycle for 180 km and then run a marathon of 42 km! **20**

Joining a club is a motivating way of training. As well as being encouraged in your sport, you meet **like-minded people**. Both boys and girls can enjoy this sport and there is no age limit.

Choose the correct answer and write its number in the brackets.

26. A triathlon is a sport for _____.
   (1)   trained experts
   (2)   anyone who can swim and cycle
   (3)   boys who can swim, run and cycle
   (4)   anyone who can swim, run and cycle   (   )

27. Triathlons became popular _____.
   (1)   in London
   (2)   in the Olympic Games
   (3)   after the Australian Olympic Games
   (4)   in clubs   (   )

28. A junior event includes _____.
    (1) a 1 km run
    (2) a 300 km swim
    (3) a 380 m swim
    (4) a 1 km cycle   (   )

29. A very good cyclist _____.
    (1) will not be racing fast at the beginning
    (2) will not buy a super racing bike
    (3) may find someone who could buy them a good bike
    (4) could sponsor others   (   )

30. The phrase 'like-minded people' in line 22 means _____.
    (1) people with the same interests
    (2) people who like running
    (3) people with one idea
    (4) people with many ideas   (   )

Section G: Grammar cloze   (10 marks)

Choose the correct word(s) from the box for each blank. Write its letter in the blank. Use each word(s) once.

A	anything	B	someone	C	why	D	which
E	yourself	F	himself	G	everyone	H	no one
J	who	K	themselves	L	herself	M	nothing
N	where	P	one another	Q	whose		

Please remember that the library is a place (31) ____N____ you can come and

work quietly. Children are not allowed to talk to (32) ____P____ here. They can,

of course, talk to the librarian. If you use a book, leave it on the table. Do not try to put it back on the shelves. Mrs Palmer, the librarian, will do this (33) _____L_____, to make sure that the books stay in the right place.

Please try to keep the library tidy. Take all your things with you when you leave. (34) _____M_____ should be left on the tables except for books. Children (35) _____Q_____ things are left in the library will have to go to the office to get them. It has been reported that (36) _____B_____ has taken a book out of the library without signing it out. (37) _____G_____ knows that this is strictly against the rules. Every book (38) _____D_____ you wish to borrow must be signed out by the librarian. You are not allowed to sign it out (39) _____F_____. If you find the book *An Untold Story*, please bring it to the library. If you know (40) _____J_____ has taken this book, please inform the librarian. The library is for all of us to use together. Please respect the rules.

Section H: Editing   (10 marks)

The words in bold have spelling errors and the underlined words are grammatical errors. Write the correct word in the box.

(41) wasn't

Ken had an accident yesterday, but luckily it <u>isn't</u> too serious. He was standing on a

(42) ladder

lader painting the windows of his house. When he reached across to paint the edge of one window, he lost his balance and fell off! Luckily, his wife was at home and she

(43) was   (44) waiting   (45) Emergency

<u>is</u> able to drive Ken to the hospital. After <u>to wait</u> at the Accident and **Emmergency**

(46) had seen   (47) X-ray

department for a while, Ken <u>was seeing</u> a doctor who took an **X-rai** of his ankle.

28

(48)	
	was

(49)	
	twisted

Luckily, nothing <u>were</u> broken. Ken had just **tweested** his ankle. Ken and his wife

(50)	
	chore

went home but Ken didn't finish his painting **choore**.

Section I: Comprehension cloze (15 marks)

Read and fill in each blank with the best word.

Everyone going on the camping holiday (51) _____is_____ advised to read these notes carefully and follow the instructions.

Please bring: a warm jumper (it (52) _____might_____ get cold at night), swimming things, including a towel, shorts and T-shirts.

We (53) _____can_____ go walking at night. If we do, you will need a torch with spare (54) _____batteries_____. Bring some games to play — outdoor games (balls, bats, etc) and indoor games like a (55) _____deck_____ of cards. Electronic games are not allowed. Any such games will (56) _____be_____ confiscated and returned to you after the trip. Everything you bring must be clearly

(57) _____labelled_____ with your name. Don't bring anything valuable or fragile.

(58) _____Any_____ money that you have should be given to the camp leader

(59) _____on_____ the first day. There will be four people in a tent. Please

(60) _____let_____ the leaders know if there are people you wish to share your

tent (61) _____them with_____. We will do our best to put you with your friends.

(62) _____If_____ you take any medicines, these must be given to the camp leaders on the first day for (63) _____safe_____ keeping.

29

Please inform the leaders of any special dietary needs.

Remember we (64) _____have to_____ leave the school car park at 8 a.m. sharp.
So don't (65) _____get_____ late!

Section J: Combining sentences   (10 marks)

Rewrite the sentence(s) using the words(s) given. Your answer must be in one sentence and its meaning must be the same as that of the given sentence(s).

66. It was raining heavily. The match was still played.

    Despite ~~it raining heavily, the match was still played.~~
    _____heavy rain, the match was still played._____

67. George moved to London three years ago.

    _____George has been in London_____
    _____ for three years.

68. The children were making a lot of noise. I didn't hear the phone ring.

    _____The children were making ~~such lot so~~_____ so much
    _____noise that I didn't hear the phone ring._____

69. If you don't hurry up, you will be late.

    _____You will be late_____ unless
    _____you hurry up._____

70. You must write the essay. You must not use a dictionary.

    _____You must write the essay_____ without
    _____using the dictionary._____

Section K: Comprehension questions   (20 marks)

Read the passage and answer the questions. Write your answers in complete sentences.

Many people work behind the scenes at a busy airport. As passengers, we only see a few of the staff who ensure an efficient airport functions as it should.

We see the check-in staff who take our luggage and give us a boarding pass, the security staff who check passports and our hand luggage, and of course, the flight attendants on the plane.   **5**

But we rarely see all the men and women who work on the runways. These people have to make sure that the runways are clear of any objects or animals. They continually check for flocks of birds that could damage a plane that is landing or taking off. This person has to scare away the birds with bangers – a type of firework. This animal control service also checks for the presence of other animals,   **10** such as snakes or dogs. Dogs can get under the fence which surrounds the airport, or may have escaped from a cage in which **they** were traveling.

In cold countries, there is a special team of people who have to clear the snow from the runways. A substance is sprayed onto the tarmac which makes the ice and snow melt. It has the same properties as salt, but it causes less damage to   **15** the planes.

71. Which three-word phrase in paragraph 1 describes a situation which is not seen?

    The 3- word phrase in paragraph 1 that describes a situation which is not seen is "behind the scenes"

31

72. What do the people who work at the check-in desks do?

They take our luggage and give our boarding pass

73. What do the people who work on the runways do?

They check the runway for any objects or animals and remove
the objects and scare away the animals with bangers

74. Who checks the hand luggage?

The security staff checks our hand luggage

75. Which word in paragraph 3 means 'groups of birds'?

The word is 'flock'.

76. Why are bangers used?

Bangers are used to scare away any animals on the runway

77. In which two ways can dogs get onto a runway?

Dogs can get onto a runway by either getting under the fence
that surrounds the airport or escape from the cage in which they
were travelling.

78. What does 'they' refer to in line 12?

'They' refers to the dogs in line 12

79. Which word in paragraph 4 means 'runway'?

The word 'tarmac' means 'runway'.

_____

80. Why is salt not used to melt ice on runways?

If salt is used, it will cause ~more~ damage to the plane ~than~ ~~it~~ ~~very high loading~~ other chemicals

Practice Paper 3

Section A: Comprehension MCQs

(5 marks)

Read the notice and answer the the questions.

Short Story Competition

Do you like writing stories?
Do you have a good imagination?
Would you like your story to be published in a magazine?
Enter our short story competition and win prizes of up to $100 in value.

The winning story in each category will be published in our magazine *A Month of Stories*.

Choose the subject of your story according to your age.

Age	Choice of title
8–10 years	The most exciting day of my life A day in the year 2020
11–13 years	The best holiday The magic pen
14–16 years	A day in the life of a dollar bill The mystery of the blue crystals

PRIZES A range of books from Publibooks's booklist, including dictionaries, encyclopedias and classic stories. Check out our website for further details of the prizes for each age group.

www.publibooks.com/short-story/prizes

Stories should be no longer than **1,000** words and should be typed.
Send your story by email to: **short-story@publibooks.com**
Don't forget to include your name and address.
Send in your entry by **31st October**.

The competition is open to US residents only. No employees of Publibooks or members of their families may enter. Proof of age may be requested.

Choose the correct answer and write its number in the brackets.

1. A story entitled 'The best holiday' can be written by someone aged
   _____.
   (1)   10
   (2)   14
   ✓(3)   12
   (4)   15   (   )

2. Who cannot enter the competition?
   (1)   an 8-year-old boy from New York
   (2)   the son of the sales director for Publibooks
   (3)   someone who has already won a competition
   (4)   a 14-year-old American girl who has had a story published   (   )

3. You should write your story _____.
   (1)   by hand
   (2)   quickly
   ✓(3)   on a computer
   (4)   without reading it through   (   )

4. If you want more information about the prizes, you should _____.
   (1)   phone Publibooks
   (2)   go to the website short-story@publibooks.com
   (3)   go to the website www.publibooks.com/short-story/prizes
   (4)   check Publibooks's booklist   (   )

5. If you enter the competition, you may have to _____.
   (1)   go to the US to collect your prize
   (2)   prove your date of birth
   (3)   write over 2,000 words
   (4)   send your entry by post   (   )

Section B: Grammar MCQs   (7 marks)

Choose the correct answer and write its number in the brackets.

6. Britain is not _____ Spain.
    (1) as hot than   (2) so hot than
    (3) as hot as   (4) hot as   (3)

7. There is an _____ view of the city from the top floor of the building.
    (1) impressed   (2) impressively
    (3) impression   (4) impressive   (4)

8. I _____ Lea since last Tuesday.
    (1) didn't see   (2) haven't saw
    (3) haven't seen   (4) didn't saw   (3)

9. I tidied away _____ books and put _____ in your room.
    (1) your/them   (2) yours/them
    (3) you/it   (4) your/it   (1)

10. None of us _____ to the park after school.
    (1) are going   (2) is go
    (3) go   (4) is going   (1)

11. When Frank was 10, he _____ to New Zealand.
    (1) was moving   (2) move
    (3) is moving   (4) moved   (4)

12. Please help _____ to some more salad.
    (1) myself   (2) herself
    (3) themselves   (4) yourself   (4)

Section C: Punctuation MCQs   (3 marks)

Read the passage. Then, choose the correct answer and write its number in the brackets.

My father (13) ◯ s birthday is on 31st December and every year I make him a calendar. Each month has a different page and I decorate each page with a photo of someone in our family. Sometimes I choose a photo that is quite funny, or I stick the photo onto a funny picture (14) ◯ so that it looks like the person is doing something strange. My father loves this present and he always puts the calendar on the wall above his desk. Do you think it's a good idea for a present (15) ◯

13. (1)   [.] full stop
     (2)   [,] comma
     (3)   [?] question mark
     (4)   ['] apostrophe   (4)

14. (1)   [.] full stop
     (2)   [,] comma
     (3)   ["] quotation marks
     (4)   [?] question mark   (2)

15. (1)   [!] exclamation mark
     (2)   [,] comma
     (3)   [?] question mark
     (4)   ['] apostrophe   (3)

Section D: Vocabulary MCQs   (5 marks)

Choose the best answer and write its number in the brackets.

16. What's for dinner? I'm absolutely _____.
     (1)   hungry   (2)   peckish
     (3)   starving   (4)   full   (3)

17. Malik was late for football practice again, so the teacher _____.
     (1)   told him on   (2)   told him of
     (3)   told him in   (4)   told him off   (4)

18. I opened the curtains and the sunlight _____ into the room.
     (1)   ran   (2)   galloped
     (3)   streamed   (4)   trickled   (3)

19. The doctor gave me a/an _____ for some medicine.
     (1)   subscription   (2)   prescription
     (3)   invitation   (4)   order   (2)

20. Please pass me the _____ of honey.
     (1)   can   (2)   packet
     (3)   jar   (4)   tube   (3)

Section E: Synonyms MCQs   (5 marks)

Read the passage. Then, choose the answer closest in meaning to the underlined word(s) and write its number in the brackets.

Sofia's work has shown (21) <u>considerable</u> progress this year. She has continued to improve in all subjects. Her results in the end-of-year examinations have been most encouraging, proving that all the hard work she has done has (22) <u>come to fruition</u>. She is a (23) <u>valued</u> member of the computer club, and is always (24) <u>willing</u> to help anyone who has a problem. She is a joy to have in the class and I wish her luck next year. I hope Sofia can continue to work (25) <u>along these lines</u> for the rest of her time at our school.

21. (1) thoughtful (2) little
    (3) a great deal of (4) worthy (?)

22. (1) produced good results (2) flowered
    (3) bloomed (4) produced food (1)

23. (1) expensive (2) priceless
    (3) important (4) worthless (3)

24. (1) pleased and ready (2) reluctant
    (3) refusing (4) cautious (1)

25. (1) on her writing (2) in this way
    (3) on the page (4) in her books (2)

Section F: Comprehension MCQs (5 marks)

Read the passage and answer the questions.

Salt is a very common but important substance. Our life depends on it. It is necessary for our bodies as it plays a role in maintaining the balance of fluid in the body. It is also one of the basic tastes we have and many people like to season their food by putting salt on it. But too much salt can be dangerous. It can cause high blood pressure and other related conditions.

5

The salt we consume comes from the sea or from rock deposits. **It** is very common these days but years ago salt was so important that it even caused wars. Years ago it was very difficult to keep food for more than a few days. Meat and fish could be smoked but there was no way of keeping food at low temperatures.

There were no fridges! When it was discovered that salt could preserve food,   **10**
it became very expensive. When the Romans heard that there was a lot of salt
in Britain, they decided that was a good reason for invading the country.

Since salt was so valuable, people started to believe that it had magical properties.
It was believed that salt could protect you from harm, so children were given a
little bag of salt to wear around their necks. It is still a superstition in many   **15**
countries that if you spill some salt it could cause bad luck, unless you throw a little
of the spilt salt over your shoulder after that.

We take salt for granted but if suddenly no more salt was available, we would
find it very hard to live.

Choose the correct answer and write its number in the brackets.

26. In the human body, salt _____.
    (1) keeps down high blood pressure
    (2) flavors food
    (3) keeps the water content balanced
    (4) causes heart disease   (3)

27. 'It' in line 6 refers to _____.
    (1) the sea
    (2) the rock
    (3) the deposits
    (4) the salt   (4)

28. Children wore a bag of salt around their necks because _____.
    (1) salt was expensive
    (2) people believed it could protect them
    (3) it was unlucky
    (4) they might spill it   (2)

29. What do people do when they spill salt?
    (1) cry
    (2) throw a little of the spilt salt over their shoulder
    (3) put it back in its container
    (4) keep quiet and pretend it never happened   (2)

30. These days salt is _____.
    (1) easily found and plentiful
    (2) harmful and difficult to find
    (3) unlucky and dangerous
    (4) rare and expensive   (1)

Section G: Grammar cloze   (10 marks)

Choose the correct word(s) from the box for each blank. Write its letter in the blank. Use each word(s) once.

A	breeds	B	escaped	C	braver	D	has emerged
E	deepest	F	bravely	G	were recaptured	H	stronger
J	strong	K	have escaped	L	deep	M	strongly
N	bravest	P	heaviest	Q	is breeding		

Severe floods in Asia have caused a lot of damage to homes and land all over Vietnam. But recently a new danger (31) ___D___ as a result of the storms. A crocodile farm which (32) ___A___ crocodiles for their skin and meat has reported that the floods have damaged the crocodile cages and many of them (33) ___K___. There were at least five thousand crocodiles on the farm, but it is not known exactly how many (34) ___B___ when the floods started two days ago.

41

Soldiers and local villagers have been (35) _____F_____ trying to hunt down the escaped crocodiles. Yesterday, ten (36) _____G_____ and two were shot. One of those shot was the (37) _____P_____ crocodile on the farm. It weighed two hundred kilograms and it needed eight people to carry it. Five of the (38) _____J_____ soldiers managed to take the recaptured crocodiles back to the farm.

It is believed that many of the crocodiles have escaped to a (39) _____L_____ lake near the farm. The authorities have (40) _____M_____ advised people not to go swimming there.

Section H: Editing   (10 marks)

The words in bold have spelling errors and the underlined words are grammatical errors. Write the correct word(s) in the box.

> (41) *despite*

Everyone knows that deserts are extremely hot and dry places. But **depsite** this,

> (42) *to grow*

giant cacti still manage growing there. How do they do this? Most plants have roots

> (43) *deep*

> (44) *shallow*

that grow deepest into the ground to find water. Cacti have very **shalow** roots.

> (45) *quickly*

These roots take in water very quick. So even though there is not much rain, almost

> (46) *absorbed*

> (47) *that*

every drop can be **adsorbed** by the roots. The water what is taken up is then

> (48) *fleshy*

transported in the plant to a storage place. The **flechy** parts of the cactus above

(49)	holds

(50)	enables

the ground <u>stores</u> this water and this **inables** the plant to survive long periods without rain.

Section I: Comprehension cloze   (15 marks)

Read and fill in each blank with the best word.

Cats are popular pets. They provide (51) ___company___ for those who live alone, but they can also be (52) ___extremely___ useful. A police force in London has adopted a 13-year- (53) ___old___ tabby cat to help in their fight against crime. This time though, the criminals (54) ___behind___ the crimes are not people, but mice.

Tiger, the tabby cat, is effective in keeping (55) ___down___ the number of mice in the police station and neighborhood. (56) ___When___ he arrived, the old building had been overrun (57) ___by___ mice, but since he has been living there, the mice (58) ___have___ disappeared. Tiger has also become a popular member of the team, and (59) ___anyone___ who works at the police station, or who visits it, has become very (60) ___fond___ of him. He is a very sociable and friendly cat (61) ___who___ likes to rub himself up against people's legs and to (62) ___be___ stroked.

Tiger used to live with an elderly woman who (63) ___had___ many friends and family, so he is used to seeing people. (64) ___When___ the elderly lady sadly died, Tiger needed a new home. Living in the police station is the ideal (65) ___place___ for Tiger.

Section J: Combining sentences (10 marks)

Rewrite the sentence(s) using the words given. Your answer must be in one sentence and its meaning must be the same as that of the given sentence(s).

66. If I were taller, I would play basketball.

    If I wasn't ────────────→ so short *I would play basketball.*

67. Eric had never seen so much snow before.

    It was the first time *Eric had seen so much snow.*

68. It rained heavily. The team won the match.

    In spite of *it raining heavily, the team won the match.*

69. I want you to finish this work by tomorrow.

    All this work *has to be finished by tomorrow* .

70. Steve resigned from his job. He wished he hadn't resigned.

    Steve regretted *his resignment from his job.*

44

Section K: Comprehension questions   (20 marks)

Read the passage and answer the questions. Write your answers in complete sentences.

Bob was driving along a quiet country road to visit his friend Anne. He had had a very tiring week and was looking forward to relaxing in the countryside. It had been a lovely summer's day and now the sun was just setting.

Bob turned on the radio and tuned in to his favorite classical music station. The beautiful music was perfect for the quiet summer countryside. When he looked   **5** up into the distance, Bob noticed something strange. A bright blue light seemed to be hovering above some trees. This part of the countryside was totally deserted. There were no farms or houses, just open fields and a few clumps of trees. He drove on towards the light.

The light became more intense as the car got nearer to **it**. Before he knew it,   **10** Bob was driving through the light. Suddenly the car stopped. Bob was surrounded by the blue light.

A few hours later, Bob woke up. It was completely dark. When Bob looked at his watch, he realized with surprise that it was 11 p.m. He had left home five hours ago. What had happened? He had no memory of anything after the car had   **15** stopped. He got out of the car and looked around him. There was nothing to see, just the road and the trees. He looked for some kind of marks or tracks, but there was nothing. Bob got back into the car and turned the key in the ignition. The engine started immediately. Bob cautiously continued his journey, feeling as though something had happened, but he couldn't explain what it was.   **20**

He realized that when he reached Anne's house, he couldn't tell her about the incident. She would only ask questions that he would not be able to answer.

He finally arrived at Anne's house 3 hours later than he had expected.
He knocked on the door and a surprised and worried Anne opened it to him.
He greeted her warmly, but did not mention the incident. He just apologized **25**
for being so late.

71. Which word in paragraph 1 means 'resting'?

   'Relaxing' means 'resting'.
   _____

72. What time of day was it when Bob was driving along the road?

   It was ~~when~~ the evening
   _____

73. How was Bob feeling?

   Bob was feeling tired.
   _____

74. Which word in paragraph 2 means staying in one place in the air?

   'Hovering' means 'staying in one place in the air'
   _____

75. What does 'it' refer to in line 10?

   'It' refers to the lights.
   _____

76. What time had Bob left home?

   Bob left home at 6 PM.

   _____

77. What happened to Bob after the car stopped?

   He was completely surrounded by blue lights and fell asleep.

   _____

78. What did Bob remember about what happened?

   He remembered that   ?

   _____

79. Why didn't Bob tell Anne about the blue light?

   Because he thought she would ask questions that he couldn't answer.

   _____

80. What do you think happened to Bob?

   I think

   _____

   I will discuss with parents

Practice Paper 4

Section A: Comprehension MCQs (5 marks)

Read the notice and answer the questions.

Learn English

Westhills Language School offers summer courses in English for students from 9–18 years of age from all over the world.

Our two-week courses are activity-packed fun opportunities to learn and enjoy yourselves.

Every morning there are English classes from 9 a.m. to 12 noon, in groups of a maximum of 8 students of the same English level, but not the same first language. You will work on oral and written skills.

Every afternoon there is a range of activities according to age group. All trips and activities are accompanied by our team leaders.

- **9–12 years old**
  games and sports, trips to Legoland, Waterworld, sights of London

- **13–15 years old**
  games and sports, trips to Alton Towers, Waterworld, sights of London

- **16–18 years old**
  trips to London museums and art galleries, shopping in London's famous markets

Every evening after dinner, there are games and quizzes, with a dance on the last evening.

Accommodation

You will stay in Westhills Manor House Boarding School, in bedrooms of 3 or 4 students per room. Meals are included with a delicious range of international food available in our self-service restaurant. The restaurant is open at mealtimes.

MORE INFORMATION AND REGISTRATION FORMS ARE AVAILABLE AT OUR WEBSITE:
www.english@westhills.uk

Choose the correct answer and write its number in the brackets.

1. You cannot attend the course if you are _____19_____ years old.
   (1) 9
   (2) 14
   (3) 18
   (4) 19   (4)

2. In the English classes, students _____.
   (1) study spoken English
   (2) are in groups of the same nationality
   (3) study spoken and written English
   (4) are in groups of over 8   (3)

3. An 11-year-old girl will not visit _____.
   (1) Waterworld
   (2) London
   (3) Alton Towers
   (4) Legoland   (3)

4. The self-service restaurant _____.
   (1) serves British food
   (2) must be paid for by the students at mealtimes
   (3) never closes
   (4) offers a choice of food from different countries   (4)

5. The team leaders _____.
   (1) study English
   (2) take the students out on trips
   (3) organize the dance
   (4) teach English   (2)

Section B: Grammar MCQs   (7 marks)

Choose the correct answer and write its number in the brackets.

6.   Bye! I _____ you later.
     (1)   am seeing   (2)   see
     (3)   will see   (4)   am going see   (3)

7.   I _____ just _____ my homework. May I go and play?
     (1)   has/finished   (2)   have/finish
     (3)   had/finished   (4)   have/finished   (4)

8.   Four families live in my block of flats. None of them _____ a dog.
     (1)   own   (2)   owns
     (3)   owning   (4)   is owning   (2)

9.   You couldn't speak English before you came here, _____?
     (1)   did you   (2)   isn't it
     (3)   couldn't you   (4)   could you   (4)

10. The library is full of books that are suitable _____ children.
     (1)   with   (2)   for
     (3)   by   (4)   from   (2)

11. Mike is meeting Ryan Khan, _____.
     (1)   actor   (2)   actors
     (3)   the actor   (4)   a actor   (3)

12. You can start the _____ activity when you have finished this one.
     (1)   each   (2)   both
     (3)   other   (4)   either   (3)

Section C: Punctuation MCQs   (3 marks)

Read the passage. Then, choose the correct answer and write its number in the brackets.

Rubik (13) ◯ s cube is a puzzle which was invented by Erno Rubik in 1974. It is a cube with many different colored tiles on its six surfaces. The aim is to move the parts of the cube until each surface has only one color (14) ◯ I am sure you have seen this game as it is said to be the world's best selling toy. In 1980, it won the German 'Game of the Year' award for the best puzzle (15) ◯

13. (1)   [.] full stop
     (2)   [,] comma
     (3)   [?] question mark
     ~~(4)~~   ['] apostrophe   (4)

14. ~~(1)~~   [.] full stop
     (2)   [,] comma
     (3)   [?] question mark
     (4)   ['] apostrophe   (1)

15. ~~(1)~~   [.] full stop
     (2)   [,] comma
     (3)   [?] question mark
     (4)   ['] apostrophe   (1)

Section D: Vocabulary MCQs   (5 marks)

Choose the best answer and write its number in the brackets.

16. Tim writes Spanish well, but his spoken Spanish is rather _____.
    (1) accurate   (2) fluent
    (3) weak   (4) flawless   (3)

17. Martina was accused of taking the money, but she _____ she was innocent.
    (1) denied   (2) claimed
    (3) told   (4) demanded   (2)

18. The horror movie was so scary I _____ when I saw the monster.
    (1) cried   (2) moaned
    (3) groaned   (4) screamed   (4)

19. Fred had an accident on his bike. He was riding fast and _____ down a hill.
    (1) recklessly   (2) roughly
    (3) rudely   (4) really   (1)

20. To make an omelette, first break two eggs into a bowl and _____ them well.
    (1) hit   (2) smack
    (3) fork   (4) beat   (4)

Section E: Synonyms MCQs   (5 marks)

Read the passage. Then, choose the answer closest in meaning to the underlined word and write its number in the brackets.

A smoke signal is a form of communication used over long distances. The smoke from a fire can be (21) underlined{interrupted} by placing a blanket over the fire. In this way (22) underlined{puffs} of smoke can be made. This form of communication was used by American Indians and the Chinese. In (23) underlined{fictional} movies about American Indians, the Indians were often (24) <u>portrayed</u> as being able to send complex messages with smoke signals. (25) <u>However</u>, this is unlikely to have really happened.

21. (1) put out   (2) paused   (2)
     (3) stepped on   (4) lit

22. (1) small amounts   (2) large amounts   (1)
     (3) cushions   (4) pieces

23. (1) factual   (2) true   (3)
     (3) untrue   (4) funny

24. (1) realized   (2) shown   (2)
     (3) produced   (4) directed

25. (1) But   (2) Also   (1)
     (3) Therefore   (4) And

Section F: Comprehension MCQs   (5 marks)

Read the passage and answer the questions.

Charles Dickens is one of Britain's best-known authors. His novels were extremely popular when they were first published and, amazingly, are still in print to this day.

Dickens was born in London in 1812 into a family of 8 children. The family was quite wealthy and Charles was sent to a private school. His father worked as a clerk earning a good salary, but unfortunately, he overspent and got into debt. **5** As a result of these debts, his father was sent to prison. When Charles was only 12, he had to leave school and earn a living to support the family. His first job was working 10 hours a day in a factory. It was here that he experienced the working conditions of many poor English people at that time.

Later, the family recovered some of their earlier wealth and Charles was able to   **10**

continue his education. He had many jobs after leaving school. He worked for

a law firm as a clerk at the law courts, and later as a journalist for a newspaper.

He started writing short stories and novels and these were published, quickly

gaining him popularity and a good income.

In 1836 Dickens married Catherine Hogarth and they lived in London. The couple   **15**

had ten children. Dickens and his wife traveled widely, visiting Canada, the USA,

Italy and Switzerland among other countries. Sadly, the marriage was not a happy

one and the couple separated in 1858. In 1865, returning from a trip to France,

the train that Dickens was traveling in was in a crash. Luckily, Dickens was unhurt.

He **tended to** the wounded passengers before the rescue services arrived at the   **20**

scene. He later used this incident in one of his stories.

Although he was not injured in the crash, Dickens never really got over it and his

health began to fail. He continued to give public readings of his best-loved books

but he wrote less and less. Dickens died five years after the crash. He was buried

in the Poets' Corner of Westminster Abbey in London.   **25**

Choose the correct answer and write its number in the brackets.

26. How many brothers and sisters did Charles Dickens have?
    (1) 7
    (2) 8
    (3) 9
    (4) 10   (ʃ)

27. Dickens' father was imprisoned because _____.
    (1) he was a clerk in an office
    (2) he owed a lot of money
    (3) he didn't earn a lot of money
    (4) Charles had to leave school   (2)

28. The phrase 'tended to' in line 20 means _____.
    (1) talked to
    (2) cared for
    (3) looked at
    (4) made notes about   (2)

29. According to the text, Dickens did not go to _____.
    (1) Italy
    (2) France
    (3) Germany
    (4) Canada   (3)

30. Dickens died _____.
    (1) in 1865
    (2) on the day of the train crash
    (3) in 1875
    (4) in 1870   (4)

Section G: Grammar cloze   (10 marks)

Choose the correct word from the box for each blank. Write its letter in the blank. Use each word once.

A	have	B	from	C	they	D	has	E	it
F	give	G	is	H	are	J	were	K	of
L	them	M	on	N	gives	P	was	Q	agrees

For our science project, our teacher has put us into groups of four. Each group

(31) _____D_____ to choose a topic from a list that the teacher has given us.

55

Every topic (32) _____ G _____ about the environment, how to protect it, how important it is, pollution and so on.

In my group, there (33) _____ P _____ a disagreement about which topic to choose, but finally we decided (34) _____ M _____ public transport.

We will interview everyone in the class and ask (35) _____ L _____ how often they use public transport, what they think about (36) _____ E _____ and whether they would like any changes. Then we will write up our results and (37) _____ S _____ will be presented to the class.

Every group (38) _____ N _____ a talk of about 10 minutes and must also hand in a written report to the teacher. It requires a lot of work, but everyone (39) _____ R _____ that it is very interesting and we will all learn a lot (40) _____ B _____ the project.

Section H: Editing   (10 marks)

The words in bold have spelling errors and the underlined words are grammatical errors. Write the correct word(s) in the box.

(41) | who |

A stunt double is a person <u>which</u> doubles for an actor in a movie. The stunt double or

(42) | does |

stunt person <u>do</u> the dangerous or very physical scenes that the actor is not allowed

(43) | is | (44) | restrictions |

to do. If the actor <u>will be</u> a child, there are **restricions** about what they are allowed

(45) | contract |

to do. If the actor is very famous, there may be conditions in their **contrak** that forbid

56

(46) doing

them from <u>do</u> anything dangerous. Stunt doubles do things such as jump out of a

(47) ride

building or **ridde** a motorbike. A stunt person can also be used to do activities that

require a lot of skill like playing a musical instrument or dancing. Some stunt doubles

(48) careers

have long **carers** doubling for the same actor in many of their movies. Other actors

(49) hiring   (50) insist

refuse <u>having</u> stunt doubles and **ensist** on doing their own stunts.

Section I: Comprehension cloze   (15 marks)

Read and fill in each blank with the best word.

A satellite is an object which moves around another larger object in space. There are

naturally occurring satellites such (51) _____as_____ the moon, and there are

many artificial ones that have (52) _____been_____ placed around the Earth by

man. Gravity is the force which holds the satellite (53) _____in_____ place as it

moves around the Earth.

The first artificial satellite was Sputnik I, which was (54) _launched_ into

space by the Soviet Union in 1957. This started the space race (55) _between_

the United States and the Soviet Union. The USA quickly developed its

(56) _____own_____ satellites and sent them into space too.

The satellites are used for different purposes. (57) _____for_____ instance, some

have a military purpose, some are for scientific (58) _____use_____ and some are

for communication technology. They are used (59) _____to_____ take photos

57

of the Earth and to help people forecast the (60) ___weather___ by observing the movement of clouds. They can (61) ___also___ give us information about possible earthquakes. Communications satellites are very (62) ___common___ these days, being used for television, cell phones and mapping devices.

Some people have asked about what is happening to (63) ___satellites___ that are no (64) ___longer___ in use. It is believed (65) ___that___ only 7% of the satellites are actually being used.

Section J: Combining sentences   (10 marks)

Rewrite the sentence(s) using the words(s) given. Your answer must be in one sentence and its meaning must be the same as that of the given sentence(s).

66. I've never heard such a funny story as that one.

    That's the _funniest story I've ever heard._

67. Jeff would love to be rich.

    Jeff wishes _he could be rich._

68. Kate lives in Germany. She moved there 5 years ago.

    Kate has _lived in Germany for 5 years._

69. "Don't make so much noise!" said the teacher.

    The teacher told the children _to not make so much noise._

70. Emily went shopping. Her sister was tidying their bedroom.

Emily went shopping ——————————————→ while
her sister was tidying her room.

Section K: Comprehension questions   (20 marks)

Read the passage and answer the questions. Write your answers in complete sentences.

Grace Darling was a heroine. She was born in 1815 in Northumberland, on the

northeast coast of England. Her father was a lighthouse keeper and Grace grew

up in a large family in a lighthouse. She never went to school, but was educated

by her parents at home.

The lighthouse was surrounded by a small patch of land where the Darling family   **5**

could grow their own food and keep some livestock: a few hens and a pig. Life was

hard, as the lighthouse was far from the town and the weather was often harsh.

In the early hours of September 7th 1838 a terrible storm was raging. A steamship,

the *Forfarshire*, sailing from Hull to Dundee developed engine problems.

The engines eventually stopped working. The ship began to move uncontrollably   **10**

and it hit a rock and broke into two.

Grace looked out of a window of the lighthouse and spotted the sinking ship

a few hundred meters from the lighthouse. She could see a few survivors clinging

to the wreckage. Grace knew that the sea was too rough for a lifeboat to go to

rescue the survivors of the shipwreck, so she and her father took a rowing boat   **15**

and rowed out to them. There were nine people in a state of terror and exhaustion waiting to be saved. But the rowing boat could only hold five of them. Grace and her father took five people and rowed them to safety. Her father then returned to rescue the remaining four.

After the accident Grace was called a heroine and she was awarded many **20** medals for bravery. She even had poems written about her. She was invited to appear at theaters around the country, but Grace was a very humble person and she refused these invitations and offers of money. She preferred to live a quiet life in the country. Sadly, she developed tuberculosis, for **which** there was no cure. She died in 1842. **25**

71. Which word in paragraph 2 means animals that are kept on a farm?

    Livestock

72. Where was the *Forfarshire* going to?

    To Dundee

73. Why did the *Forfarshire* break up?

    Because it started moving uncontrollably and hit a rock.

74. Why didn't a lifeboat go to rescue the survivors?

    Because the sea was too rough for the lifeboat.

75. How were the nine shipwrecked people feeling as they waited to be rescued?

They were feeling terrified and exhausted.

76. Why didn't Grace and her father save all nine survivors at the same time?

Because the boat could only hold 5 people.

77. What was Grace given after the rescue?

She was given many medals, and invitations to appear at different theatres around the country.

78. Why didn't Grace appear on stage?

Because she wanted to live a quiet life in the country.

79. What is 'tuberculosis'?

Tuberculosis is a disease of the lungs which had no cure.

80. What does 'which' refer to in line 24?

Tuberculosis.

Practice Paper 5

Section A: Comprehension MCQs

(5 marks)

Read the notice and answer the questions.

Come and join our Drama Club!

We are looking for enthusiastic boys and girls between the ages of 10 and 14 to join our theater group. No experience in acting is required. You just need to be keen and outgoing.

Do you like acting? Come and chat with us next Tuesday and find out what we do. There will be a chance to meet our current members, watch a few sketches and hear more about our projects for this year.

Our end-of-year play will be based on a well-known folk story that everyone loves. There are many roles to fill! We need actors for star parts and smaller parts, as well as non-speaking extras. Backstage help is always important in any play and we welcome anyone who would like to help out behind the scenes. We will find everyone a useful job. (At the moment only the director's job is not vacant.)

We meet every Tuesday evening from September to April. In May there will be rehearsals on some weekends. Our play will be shown on three dates in June.

A small joining fee will be payable if you decide to join. The first two sessions are free.

Choose the correct answer and write its number in the brackets.

1. To join the Drama Club you need to _____.
    (1) be over 14
    (2) have already acted
    (3) be kind and pleasant
    (4) be enthusiastic   (4)

2. Next Tuesday there will be _____.
    (1) a performance of a full-length play
    (2) a chance to talk to people already in the club
    (3) a chance to act in a short play
    (4) a request for ideas for next year   (2)

3. For the play, the club doesn't need _____.
    (1) backstage help
    (2) actors and actresses
    (3) people who don't want speaking roles
    (4) a director   (4)

4. From September to April, the Drama Club meets _____.
    (1) every weekend
    (2) once a week
    (3) three times a week
    (4) on some weekends   (2)

5. To join the Drama Club you _____.
    (1) don't have to pay anything
    (2) have to pay a large sum of money
    (3) have to pay for each session
    (4) have to pay a small amount of money   (4)

Section B: Grammar MCQs   (7 marks)

Choose the correct answer and write its number in the brackets.

6.   The teacher complimented the children _____ their excellent
     test results.
     (1) on   (2) of
     (3) because   (4) by   (1)

7.   You _____ go to bed early tonight. You've got a busy day tomorrow.
     (1) may   (2) should to
     (3) ought to   (4) have   (3)

8.   Glass bottles _____ in most countries.
     (1) are recycling   (2) is recycled
     (3) recycle   (4) are recycled   (2)

9.   I'm exhausted! I _____ hard all day.
     (1) have be worked   (2) has been worked
     (3) have being worked   (4) have been working   (4)

10. The latest Spyman story was not _____ the last one.
     (1) as good than   (2) as good
     (3) as good as   (4) good as   (3)

11. Bring _____ friends and family to the school carnival.
     (1) you   (2) yours
     (3) their   (4) your   (4)

12. Vincent refused _____ me with my homework.
     (1) helping   (2) to help
     (3) help   (4) helped   (2)

Read the passage. Then, choose the correct answer and write its number in the brackets.

Yesterday, when I was walking home, someone stopped me in the street. "Excuse me (13) ◯ the man said. "I was wondering if you could help me (14) ◯ I'm looking for the nearest post office. Could you tell me where it is?" Of course I knew where the post office was, but it was not easy to explain how to get there. In fact it took me several minutes to try to explain. In the end I got out a piece of paper and drew the man a map. He was very grateful and we went our separate ways. It was only when I got home that I realized the man had gone off with my pen. In fact it wasn't even my pen. It was my brother (15) ◯ s .

13. (1) [!] exclamation mark
    (2) [,"] comma and quotation marks
    (3) [?"] question mark and quotation marks
    (4) ["] quotation marks

    (3 or 4)

14. (1) [.] full stop
    (2) [,] comma
    (3) [?] question mark
    (4) ['] apostrophe

    (3)

15. (1) [!] exclamation mark
    (2) [,] comma
    (3) ["] quotation marks
    (4) ['] apostrophe

    (4)

Section D: Vocabulary MCQs   (5 marks)

Choose the best answer and write its number in the brackets.

16. I hope this cut on my finger _____ soon.
    (1) cures   (2) treats
    (3) heals   (4) scars   (3)

17. Mark works full time and still is able to study by taking a night _____.
    (1) train   (2) lesson
    (3) letter   (4) class   (2)

18. This T-shirt was my size, but I washed it in very hot water and now it has
    _____ and is too tight.
    (1) faded   (2) dyed
    (3) shrunk   (4) disappeared   (3)

19. These flowers have a lovely _____.
    (1) odor   (2) breath
    (3) stench   (4) fragrance   (4)

20. Someone left the _____ of ice cream on the table. Now it's all melted.
    (1) bottle   (2) tub
    (3) tube   (4) tin   (2)

Section E: Synonyms MCQs   (5 marks)

Read the passage. Then, choose the answer closest in meaning to the underlined word(s) and write its number in the brackets.

When Penny opened the door to her room, she realized immediately that someone had been there. The papers on her desk were not in the tidy order she had left them and someone had been (21) messing with her magazines. Instead of being in a neat pile, they were (22) scattered over the floor. There was a (23) distinct mark in the bed cover as if someone had been lying on the bed. A movement of the floor-length curtain

66

caught her eye. Was there still someone in the room? (24) <u>Trembling</u>, Penny went to the curtain and (25) <u>drew it back</u> quickly. Behind the curtain, Mog the cat was sitting and licking her paw.

21. (1) re-ordering   (2) untidying
     (3) tidying   (4) cleaning   (2)

22. (1) spread   (2) heaped
     (3) sorted   (4) ordered   (1)

23. (1) smudged   (2) blurred
     (3) clear   (4) soft   (3)

24. (1) laughing   (2) crying
     (3) shaking   (4) scaring   (3)

25. (1) painted it   (2) opened it
     (3) closed it   (4) pulled it down   (2)

Section F: Comprehension MCQs   (5 marks)

Read the passage and answer the questions.

Serendipity is the chance discovery of something while looking for something else. The word comes from an old, Persian fairy tale called the *Three Princes of Serendip*.

Three princes were looking for a camel. They made observations and conclusions about this camel by examining its tracks. They decided that it was blind in one   **5** eye because the grass had only been eaten on one side of the road. They also said that it was missing a tooth, carrying a pregnant lady, and loaded with butter on one side and honey on the other.

Because they were so clever, they were accused of stealing the camel and were sentenced to death. Just before the punishment was to be carried out, a traveler appeared and informed everyone that he had seen the camel wandering in the desert. The lives of the princes were saved and they were given many riches for their cleverness. These rewards were not expected or looked for, and so were serendipitous.

There are many examples of serendipity in science. Scientists have discovered things when they were actually looking for something else. For example, the antibiotic penicillin was discovered by chance, by Alexander Fleming. He had left some bacteria in his laboratory and he noticed that **it** had got contaminated with a fungus. He then realized that the fungus was actually producing something that was killing the bacteria. Later the substance was purified, and so the first antibiotic was discovered.

Safety glass was invented when a French scientist accidentally knocked a glass flask onto the ground. Instead of spreading out onto the floor, the glass pieces were held together by a liquid plastic that had formed a thin film in the glass.

Ideas that have come to people in dreams, or when thinking about something else, are also called serendipitous. Serendipity is a concept that is quite difficult to explain and it has been said that it is one of the most difficult words to translate into other languages.

10

15

20

25

Choose the correct answer and write its number in the brackets.

26. The three princes decided that the camel was blind in one eye because
_____.
    (1) they saw it walking with a heavy load
    (2) the camel kept walking into things
    (3) it only ate grass from the side it could see
    (4) it only had one eye   (3)

27. The princes were not put to death because _____.
    (1) it was a serendipitous result
    (2) the camel was seen walking around
    (3) they had stolen the camel
    (4) they were given gifts   (2)

28. The word 'it' in line 18 refers to _____.
    (1) the laboratory
    (2) the bacteria
    (3) a fungus
    (4) penicillin   (2)

29. The French scientist got the idea for safety glass when _____.
    (1) broken pieces of glass spread over the floor
    (2) broken pieces of glass were held together
    (3) a thin film of plastic spread over the floor
    (4) a dropped flask did not break   (2)

30. Serendipity _____.
    (1) does not exist in other languages
    (2) is an easy idea
    (3) is easy to say in other languages
    (4) is not easy to translate   (4)

Section G: Grammar cloze

(10 marks)

Choose the correct word(s) from the box for each blank. Write its letter in the blank. Use each word(s) once.

A using	B to use	C reminding	D any	E to check
F see	G other	H some	J checking	K neither
L to remind	M seeing	N respecting	P no	Q respect

It has come to our notice that (31) ___H___ students are not aware of the rules concerning the use of the school's computer facilities. We would like (32) ___L___ all students that, as is stated in the Rules, Section 2.4, under (33) ___P___ circumstances may computers be used for personal emails. (34) ___K___ can school time be spent surfing the Internet for anything (35) ___G___ than school-related purposes. Teachers have been instructed (36) ___E___ on the use of computers by all their students and to make a note of (37) ___D___ student who does not respect these rules. Students found (38) ___A___ computers for their own personal reasons may not be allowed to enter the computer room. (39) ___N___ the rules of the school is important and ensures that our school runs effectively. We look forward to (40) ___M___ an improvement soon.

Section H: Editing   (10 marks)

The words in bold have spelling errors and the underlined words are grammatical errors. Write the correct word in the box.

(41) showing

A compass is an instrument for <u>show</u> direction. It is made of a magnetized pointer

(42) which

(43) magnetic

<u>what</u> can move freely. This pointer lines itself up with the Earth's **magnetik** north

(44) that

and <u>so that</u> indicates the direction of north. The invention of this instrument made it

(45) navigate

much easier for ships to find their way, or **navagate**. Before compasses, ships found

(46) rubbing

their way by using the stars. It is possible to make a very simple compass by **rubing**

(47) piece

a needle on a **peace** of silk. This makes the needle magnetic. If you put the needle in

(48) float

a short straw and **flote** it in some water, the needle will move so that it points to the

north. Some animals use the Earth's magnetic field to find their way, but it is not

(49) known

(50) do

<u>knowing</u> exactly how the animals <u>does</u> this.

71

Section I: Comprehension cloze (15 marks)

Read and fill in each blank with the best word.

An escalator is a moving staircase which was designed to transport people
(51) _____from_____ one level to another. There are many advantages to
(52) _____this_____. They can be used almost anywhere (underground, outside,
in shopping centers), they (53) _____can_____ transport large numbers of people
with no waiting time (except (54) _____during_____ busy periods) and they only use
the same space as a staircase.

Usually, escalators (55) _____?_____ in pairs, with one going up and the other
going (56) _____down_____. In some places however, there are no escalators
going down.

(57) _____There_____ are guidelines about how to use them. Usually if
(58) _____you_____ wish to stand still, you stay on one side, leaving the
(59) _____other_____ side free for those who wish to walk. The side
(60) _____of_____ standing is not the same as the side of the road on
(61) _____which_____ people drive. In London, Boston and Hong Kong,
people stand on (62) _____the_____ right and walk on the left. Whereas
in Singapore, Australia (63) _____and_____ New Zealand, they stand
on the left. In some countries there are no rules and people randomly stand on
(64) _____any_____ side. In Montreal, in Canada, it is forbidden to walk
(65) _____on_____ escalators.

Section J: Combining sentences   (10 marks)

Rewrite the sentence(s) using the words(s) given. Your answer must be in one sentence and its meaning must be the same as that of the given sentence(s).

66. Jack felt unwell. Jack sat for his final exam.

Although _Jack felt unwell, he sat for his final exam_

_____

67. Kate had never seen such a beautiful dress.

It was the _most beautiful dress Kate had seen._

_____

68. The Romans built the road almost 2,000 years ago.

The road _was built by the romans almost 2,000 years_
ago.

69. The temperature will rise slightly tomorrow.

There will be _a slight rise in temperature tomorrow_

_____

70. You don't try hard. You won't be picked for the team.

Unless _you try hard, you won't be picked for the team._

_____

73

Section K: Comprehension questions (20 marks)

Read the passage and answer the questions. Write your answers in complete sentences.

A nursery rhyme is a poem or song that is told to young children. Nursery rhymes are traditionally told to children by their parents to entertain them, or to calm them before they go to sleep; but they also teach them words and numbers.

The origins of nursery rhymes are sometimes difficult to trace as they date back to hundreds of years ago.   **5**

> *Mary had a little lamb*
> *Its fleece was white as snow*
> *And everywhere that Mary went*
> *The lamb was sure to go.*

'Mary Had a Little Lamb', was a poem originally published by Sarah Hale in **10**
1830. It was based on a true incident in which a little girl called Mary Sawyer kept a pet lamb. The lamb loved Mary and followed her around the farm where she lived. One day, Mary took the lamb to school. Naturally, this caused a lot of excitement. A young man, John Roulstone, who was visiting the school enjoyed this so much that the next day he wrote the first few verses of the poem. But it is **15**
not clear whether Sarah Hale wrote the remaining verses or whether the young man wrote all of them.

> *Ring a ring o' roses,*
> *A pocketful of posies.*

74

Ah-tishoo! Ah-tishoo!   **20**
We all fall down.

'Ring a Ring of Roses' is often connected with the Great Plague of London. The poem refers to flowers in a pocket, and people falling down. This shows people falling ill and dying from the plague. The plague was an illness that spread rapidly from 1665 to 1666 in London. At that time the city was a very   **25** dirty place and people did not understand the importance of keeping clean. The plague killed many people. At its worst period 7,000 people died in one week. It has been estimated that around 100,000 people died from the plague in England. It was not known how people got the disease and it was thought that bad smells caused it. So people believed that you could protect yourself by   **30** putting something sweet-smelling, like some flowers, in your pocket.

Humpty Dumpty sat on a wall.
Humpty Dumpty had a great fall.
All the king's horses and all the king's men
Couldn't put Humpty together again.   **35**

The rhyme 'Humpty Dumpty' was written as a puzzle or riddle. Humpty Dumpty fell off a wall, but why was he so badly hurt that 'all the king's horses and all the king's men' couldn't make him better? Of course, we now know that he was not a person, but an egg.

Traditionally these rhymes were not written down but were just said. As a result,   **40** it is certain that many of **them** have been lost.

71. Why do parents tell their children nursery rhymes?

To entertain them or calm them down before they sleep.

72. Which word in the rhyme 'Mary Had a Little Lamb' means the wool coat of a lamb?

Fleece

73. Who was Mary Sawyer?

Mary Sawyer was a little girl who inspired the poem "Mary had a little lamb".

74. What happened when Mary took the lamb to school with her?

When Mary took the lamb to school, there was a lot of excitement and a young man was inspired to write the first few verses of the poem "Mary had a little lamb".

75. Do we know who wrote the poem 'Mary Had a Little Lamb'?

John Roulstone and Sarah Hale wrote the poem 'Mary had a little lamb'.

76. How many people died from the plague in England?

Over 100000

77. Why did people carry flowers in their pocket in the 17th century?

Because they thought bad smell caused the disease and good-smelling items ~~that~~ protected them from the disease

78. What happened to Humpty Dumpty?

He fell off a wall and broke his shell and even the kingsmen and horses could not put him back together.

79. What does 'them' refer to in line 41?

'Nursery rhymes'

80. Why have some nursery rhymes been lost?

~~Because over cente it has been changed so much that the original we~~

Because these ~~so~~ rhymes were not written down, they were just said.

Practice Paper 6

Section A: Comprehension MCQs

(5 marks)

Read the notice and answer the questions.

The Institute of Science and Technology Open Day

Program

Everyone is welcome to attend our fifth annual open day on 30th September. Please read the program carefully.

You may choose which events to attend. Entrance to lectures and talks is 5 minutes before the starting time. No one can enter after the speaker has started. We thank you for your understanding and wish you all an exciting day.

Time	Event	
9.00	Welcome speech by the President Dr J. Lee *Isaac Newton Lecture Theater, Main building*	
9.30–10.30	Guided tour of the main building	
10.30–10.45	Coffee break *Reception area, Main building*	
10.45–11.45	Physics Today (Talks and demonstrations from the Physics department) *Isaac Newton Lecture Theater, Main building*	Chemistry in Our Lives (Demonstrations and displays) *Sanger Room,* *Chemistry Department*
12.00–1.30	Lunch *Cafeteria, Main building*	
1.30–3.00	IT developments (Lecture by Professor Hirsch) *Seminar room,* *Computer Science Department*	Building Bridges (Talks and Exhibitions) *Brunel Lecture Theater,* *Engineering Department*
3.15–4.00	Science in the 21st Century (Public Debate led by Professor B. Boax. The public are invited to participate.) *Isaac Newton Lecture Theater, Main building*	

Choose the correct answer and write its number in the brackets.

1. To listen to a lecture you must arrive _____.
   (1) after the lecturer has begun his/her talk
   (2) at the same time as the speaker
   (3) before the lecturer begins his/her talk
   (4) any time you choose   (   )

2. Which of the following events is held in the lecture theater in the main building?
   (1) Chemistry in Our Lives
   (2) Coffee break
   (3) Public Debate
   (4) Talks and Exhibitions   (   )

3. At 11.15 you could be listening to _____.
   (1) a lecture by Professor Hirsh
   (2) a talk about Building Bridges
   (3) a lecture in the Chemistry department
   (4) a talk about Physics Today   (   )

4. The Open Day is held _____.
   (1) from 9 a.m. to 5 p.m.
   (2) every year
   (3) very 5 years
   (4) in only one building   (   )

5. The final event is a(n) _____.
   (1) talk
   (2) demonstration
   (3) exhibition
   (4) debate   (   )

Section B: Grammar MCQs   (7 marks)

Choose the correct answer and write its number in the brackets.

6. _____ you mind if I opened the window?
   (1) Could   (2) Should
   (3) Would   (4) May   (   )

7. The mail _____ this morning. I wonder why not.
   (1) wasn't delivered   (2) weren't delivered
   (3) wasn't delivering   (4) wasn't deliver   (   )

8. The room wasn't _____ to hold the meeting.
   (1) enough large   (2) too large
   (3) large enough   (4) enough largely   (   )

9. Jane has lost her watch. Her parents gave _____ to _____
   for her birthday.
   (1) her/it   (2) them/she
   (3) her/she   (4) it/her   (   )

10. You would feel better if you _____ some fresh air.
    (1) getting   (2) would get
    (3) will get   (4) got   (   )

11. What are the main differences _____ alligators and crocodiles?
    (1) with   (2) between
    (3) from   (4) than   (   )

12. We're going on holiday tomorrow. I feel really _____.
    (1) exciting   (2) excite
    (3) excited   (4) excitement   (   )

80

Section C: Punctuation MCQs   (3 marks)

Read the passage. Then, choose the correct answer and write its number in the brackets.

"Good morning everyone!" the teacher greeted the students in her usual way.
(13) ◯ I'd like you to get out your English books for a surprise spelling test."
The children (14) ◯ s faces fell but they got out their books and prepared to write
what the teacher dictated to them. The test had ten words that they had learned
last week, including some difficult ones (15) ◯ separate, majestic, justice and
disappointing.

13. (1) [!] exclamation mark
     (2) [,] comma
     (3) [?] question mark
     (4) ["] quotation marks   (   )

14. (1) [!] exclamation mark
     (2) [,] comma
     (3) [?] question mark
     (4) ['] apostrophe   (   )

15. (1) [!] exclamation mark
     (2) [,] comma
     (3) [?] question mark
     (4) [:] colon   (   )

Section D: Vocabulary MCQs   (5 marks)

Choose the best answer and write its number in the brackets.

16. Steve Robinson _____ taking part in the robbery.
    (1) claimed   (2) insisted
    (3) denied   (4) reported   (   )

17. It was a clear night and thousands of stars were _____ in the sky.
    (1) sparking   (2) lighting
    (3) flashing   (4) twinkling   (   )

18. The car accident was caused by the wet and _____ surface of
    the road.
    (1) sliding   (2) slippery
    (3) skating   (4) spilling   (   )

19. Which _____ of ice cream is your favorite?
    (1) perfume   (2) favor
    (3) taste   (4) flavor   (   )

20. She said she was sorry, but she did not sound _____.
    (1) convincing   (2) connecting
    (3) concerning   (4) convince   (   )

Section E: Synonyms MCQs   (5 marks)

Read the passage. Then, choose the answer closest in meaning to the underlined word and write its number in the brackets.

Alice left the office at 6 o'clock and started to walk home. The sky was dark and the
heavy clouds were (21) threatening rain. It looked like a storm was (22) brewing.
Suddenly a flash of lightning lit up the sky, along with a crack of thunder and the first
fat drops of rain fell. Alice quickened her (23) pace and turned up the collar of her
coat. She wished she had brought her umbrella with her. The rain became heavier

and Alice (24) <u>sought</u> somewhere she could shelter until the storm passed. A little further up the road the welcoming lights of a café shone onto the pavement. Alice hurried on. (25) <u>Gratefully</u>, she let herself into the café and sat down at one of the tables.

21.　(1)　full of　　　　　　　(2)　complete
　　　(3)　warning of　　　　 (4)　falling　　　　　　　　　(　　)

22.　(1)　developing　　　　 (2)　dying
　　　(3)　passing　　　　　　 (4)　finishing　　　　　　　 (　　)

23.　(1)　thoughts　　　　　　(2)　speed
　　　(3)　mind　　　　　　　　(4)　package　　　　　　　 (　　)

24.　(1)　wanted　　　　　　　(2)　thought
　　　(3)　tried to find　　　 (4)　saw　　　　　　　　　　 (　　)

25.　(1)　Desperately　　　　 (2)　Thoughtfully
　　　(3)　Sadly　　　　　　　 (4)　Thankfully　　　　　　 (　　)

Section F: Comprehension MCQs   (5 marks)

Read the passage and answer the questions.

Genetically Modified Organisms, or GMOs, are living things whose genetic material has been changed in some way. The genetic material of an organism carries all the information necessary for the living thing to develop and survive.

Genetic modification has been used to develop medicines and to understand and treat human diseases.

5

GMOs have been produced to help the environment. Some bacteria have been developed that can remove a poisonous substance like mercury from water. So these GMOs can help us in the fight against pollution.

GM animals have been used in research to enable scientists to understand the effects of changes. Fruit flies are used in such experiments because they can   **10** be grown in the laboratory easily and their genetic material is simpler than other animals.

Genetically modified plants have been developed and are said to be better than the unmodified species. They can grow faster, or are more resistant to diseases, or produce more food for people. But not everyone agrees that GMOs are a   **15** good thing.

Some people believe that it is not natural to change living things in these ways and it cannot be good for the environment. Others fear that scientists do not yet know all the possible consequences that these changes may have.

Some countries in the world have banned GMOs from being used. They do not   **20** allow the import of food made from GMOs. Other countries have passed laws ensuring that all **such food** must be clearly labeled so that consumers know exactly what they are buying.

It is not yet clear whether GMOs are useful or not. At the moment, all we can say for sure is that time will tell.   **25**

Choose the correct answer and write its number in the brackets.

26. According to the text, genetic modification has not been used in _____.
    (1) research on diseases
    (2) treating pollution in the environment
    (3) developing plants for food
    (4) keeping flies off food   (   )

27. Genetic modification has not helped with _____.
    (1) developing medicine
    (2) increasing salaries
    (3) pollution
    (4) food production   (   )

28. Fruit flies are used in experiments because they _____.
    (1) are easy to grow
    (2) are complex organisms
    (3) live on fruit
    (4) cause diseases   (   )

29. Some people are against GMOs because _____.
    (1) they are expensive to produce
    (2) they absorb toxins from water
    (3) their effect on the environment is not known
    (4) they produce cheap food   (   )

30. The phrase 'such food' in line 22 refers to _____.
    (1) imported food
    (2) food made from GMOs
    (3) food from plants
    (4) food in supermarkets   (   )

Section G: Grammar cloze

Choose the correct word(s) from the box for each blank. Write its letter in the blank. Use each word(s) once.

A had	B see	C was
D have	E absolutely	F go
G is	H would drive	J would you like
K very	L if	M will you like
N rather	P would you go	Q closed

If you could go anywhere in the world, where (31) _____? My dream trip would be to go to the USA. If I (32) _____ enough time (and money), I would start my trip in New York and visit the (33) _____ famous sights there. After New York, I would go to Washington and (34) _____ the museums, like the National Air and Space Museum. I would love to go to Florida and (35) _____ to the many attraction parks. I think visiting Disney World would be (36) _____ thrilling. It must be hard to choose which rides to go on! After Florida, I (37) _____ across the States to California and see the sights of the San Francisco Bay Area. I would go to the beach (38) _____ the weather (39) _____ good. I can just see myself lying in the sun relaxing. (40) _____ to go to the USA too?

Section H: Editing

The words in bold have spelling errors and the underlined words are grammatical errors. Write the correct word in the box.

My grandfather always wore the same jacket when he went out. It was an old cotton

(41) [   ]   (42) [   ]

jacket with patches **sown** onto the elbows where the material had <u>wear</u> through.

(43) [   ]

My grandmother always wanted him to buy a new one but he refused, <u>say</u> his old one

(44) [   ]

was good **enugh**. One day, they received an invitation to tea from their neighbors

(45) [   ]

for the following weekend and my grandmother insisted that Grandpa should <u>to buy</u>

(46) [   ]

a new jacket for the **ocassion**. They went to the large department store in town and

(47) [   ]

Grandpa tried on many different jackets. None of them <u>were</u> quite right. One was too

(48) [   ]

long in the **slieves**, the other was too short. Another was too heavy, another too light.

But finally, Grandpa tried on a jacket and said, "This is the perfect one. I will

(49) [   ]

<u>bought</u> it."

(50) [   ]

"I'm sorry," the shop **assistent** said. I cannot sell you that jacket. It is your old one."

87

Section I: Comprehension cloze   (15 marks)

Read and fill in each blank with the best word.

Australia is the largest island in the world. Since it is (51) _____ isolated
island, some of the animals and plants that live (52) _____ are unique
to the country. Koalas and kangaroos are typical animals that we connect
(53) _____ Australia. They are marsupials, this means that the females
of these mammals (54) _____ a pouch or bag, in which they carry the
young (55) _____.

Kangaroos are quite large animals and they need a (56) _____ of food.
They can cause a lot of damage to farmers' (57) _____ as they easily
jump over fences to feed on the plants (58) _____ in the fields. So, for
many years, farmers have been developing (59) _____ to protect their
crops from these kangaroos. They have recently (60) _____ that roos
are scared of their own noise. When kangaroos sense danger they thump
(61) _____ feet and this signals to other roos that danger is near
and they (62) _____ off. When the farmers play a recording of
foot thumping, it has the same effect and the roos run (63) _____.
It (64) _____ hoped that this technique can be used to keep kangaroos
(65) _____ from busy roads, as sadly, many of them are run over
and killed.

Section J: Combining sentences   (10 marks)

Rewrite the sentence(s) using the words(s) given. Your answer must be in one sentence and its meaning must be the same as that of the given sentence(s).

66. "Unless it stops raining, we won't go for a walk," said Paul.

    Paul said _____

    _____

67. The display of flowers in the reception area was amazing.

    I was _____

    _____

68. You should visit the new exhibition at the museum.

    It's worth _____

    _____

69. Jenny washed up the dishes. Her mother had a rest.

    Jenny _____ so that

    _____

70. The photocopier is being repaired. You can't use the photocopier.

    _____ because

    _____

Section K: Comprehension questions   (20 marks)

Read the passage and answer the questions. Write your answers in complete sentences.

Sam was fed up with doing homework. He had been stuck indoors working all morning and it was such a lovely day outside. He had only a few more math sums to do and he raced through them without checking them properly. "Too bad," he thought to himself. "I have had enough of math."

He went into the kitchen, where his mother was unpacking the shopping.   **5**

"Could you give me a hand, Sam?" asked his mother.

"Do I have to?" replied Sam rudely. "I want to go for a bike ride. I've been working all morning."

"Well, we can't always do what we want!" snapped his mother.

Sam left his mother and went to the garage where his father was cleaning the car. **10**
"Could you get me the vacuum cleaner, Sam?" asked his father.

"No, I can't!" and before his father could scold him, Sam grabbed his bike and set off down the road. He knew he had been rude, but he felt that he deserved some time to enjoy himself. Why should he always have to help out at home?

Sam raced his bike along the country road and off onto a track that led   **15**
into the woods. The sun was shining and he could hear the birds singing in the trees. He cycled on and on, turning right or left onto different paths.

After about an hour, Sam noticed that his bike was really hard to cycle. What
was wrong? He got off and looked at the tires. To his dismay, he saw that he had
a puncture. Normally he always took a repair kit with him, but today he had left **20**
home in a temper and had taken nothing. As he looked around he realized that
he wasn't sure where he was. This part of the woods didn't look very familiar.

He turned his bike around and started to push it back along the path. When he
came to a fork, he couldn't decide which way to turn. Right or left? He looked for
tracks in the dirt but there were so many he couldn't tell which ones were from his **25**
bike. He turned left and continued to push his bike along the path.

On and on he pushed until he came to a clearing and sat down on a tree stump,
letting his bike fall onto the ground. He realized that he was lost. No one knew
where he was. Tears began to prick his eyes. If only he hadn't stormed off like
that. He hadn't told anyone where he was going, and now no one would ever **30**
find him.

After what seemed like ages, Sam heard some voices and laughter. The noises
were getting closer. He stood up and looked around him. Coming his way were
some boys on their bikes. He stood on the path and shouted to them.

"Can you help me?" he asked shyly. "I've got a puncture and I can't find my way **35**
home." The boys told Sam that he was only a few minutes from his home. They
gave him directions and in no time, Sam was pushing his bike up the garden path
to his house.

His father came out to greet him. "Are you alright?" he asked. "We were getting
worried about you." **40**

"Yes I'm fine now, thank you. But my bike has a puncture. And I'm sorry I was rude to you earlier."

"Yes, we were rather surprised that you should answer back like that. But never mind. Would you like some help mending the puncture?"

Sam thought carefully before replying. "Thank you, but I think I should try to do it **45** on my own."

71. Why didn't Sam finish his homework properly?

_____

_____

72. Why didn't Sam want to help his parents?

_____

_____

73. In what manner did Sam leave his house?

_____

_____

74. After cycling along the country road, where did Sam go?

_____

_____

75. What made Sam get off his bike and notice the flat tire?

_____

_____

76. Why hadn't Sam taken a repair kit with him?

_____

_____

77. Why couldn't he follow the tracks of his bike to find his way home?

_____

_____

78. Why do you think Sam sat down in the clearing?

_____

_____

_____

79. What regrets did Sam have while he was sitting in the clearing?

_____

_____

_____

80. Why do you think Sam didn't accept his father's offer to help mend the puncture?

_____

_____

_____

Practice Paper 7

Section A: Comprehension MCQs   (5 marks)

Read the notice and answer the questions.

Swindon	Bath	Bristol	Newport	Cardiff
Time				
* 07.05	—	07.45	08.02	08.23
⊗ 07.35	08.05	08.20	08.37	08.57
* 08.05	—	08.45	09.02	09.23
* 08.35	09.05	09.20	09.37	09.57
* 09.05	—	09.45	10.02	10.23
+ 09.10	09.40	09.55	10.12	10.32

⊗ Trains run every day of the week, every day of the year

* Trains run Mondays–Fridays, except public holidays

+ Sundays and public holidays only

Choose the correct answer and write its number in the brackets.

1. If John has an appointment in Bath at 9 o'clock on Monday morning,
    which is the latest train he can take from Swindon?
    (1) 07.05
    (2) 07.35
    (3) 08.05
    (4) 08.35   (   )

2. On Sundays, when does the first train arrive at Newport?
    (1) 08.02
    (2) 08.37
    (3) 09.02
    (4) 10.12   (   )

3. How long does the train take to travel from Bristol to Cardiff?
    (1) about 37 minutes
    (2) about 23 minutes
    (3) 57 minutes
    (4) about 50 minutes   (   )

4. If you live in Newport and work every weekday in Cardiff, which is
    the latest train you can take to arrive in Cardiff before half past nine in
    the morning?
    (1) 09.02
    (2) 08.37
    (3) 08.35
    (4) 08.05   (   )

5. How many trains stop in Bath on public holidays?
    (1) 3
    (2) 2
    (3) 1
    (4) 4   (   )

Section B: Grammar MCQs (7 marks)

Choose the correct answer and write its number in the brackets.

6. You didn't come by bus, _____?
   (1) didn't you   (2) did you
   (3) do you   (4) don't you   (   )

7. Mark was hungry at 10 o'clock, even though he _____ a big breakfast.
   (1) has had   (2) had had
   (3) have had   (4) has having   (   )

8. The library was closed. There was _____ there.
   (1) everyone   (2) anyone
   (3) someone   (4) no one   (   )

9. Jasmine _____ rather play outside than watch television.
   (1) could   (2) may
   (3) would   (4) might   (   )

10. Do you believe _____ ghosts?
    (1) in   (2) on
    (3) for   (4) of   (   )

11. Mary was running so fast _____ she got a pain in her side.
    (1) because   (2) because of
    (3) that   (4) result   (   )

12. Please hurry up. I _____ the shop.
    (1) about to close   (2) will close
    (3) close   (4) am about to close   (   )

Section C: Punctuation MCQs (3 marks)

Read the passage. Then, choose the correct answer and write its number in the brackets.

In a lifetime, a person will spend about a year looking for things they have lost.

The things that people lose most frequently are umbrellas, keys and cell phones.

Most public transport systems have a lost and found office, where objects that

have been left on trains or in stations are kept until their owners claim them.

London (13) ◯ s lost property office deals with about 130,000 items a year.

The most common items are bags and cell phones (14) ◯ Among the more unusual

things to be left on the London underground are a wedding dress and a kitchen

sink (15) ◯

13. (1) [.] full stop
    (2) [,] comma
    (3) [?] question mark
    (4) ['] apostrophe   (   )

14. (1) [.] full stop
    (2) [,] comma
    (3) [?] question mark
    (4) ["] quotation marks   (   )

15. (1) [!] exclamation mark
    (2) [,] comma
    (3) [?] question mark
    (4) ["] quotation marks   (   )

Section D: Vocabulary MCQs

Choose the best answer and write its number in the brackets.

16. When the girls saw Mrs Lopez's funny hat, they couldn't help _____.
    (1) googling   (2) gurgling
    (3) giggling   (4) gargling   (   )

17. The tennis ball hit the window and _____ it.
    (1) creaked   (2) crashed
    (3) croaked   (4) cracked   (   )

18. Hang your coat up. Don't leave it in a _____ on the floor.
    (1) heap   (2) stack
    (3) lump   (4) row   (   )

19. I've _____ my glasses. Could you help me find them, please?
    (1) misused   (2) misplaced
    (3) mistaken   (4) misled   (   )

20. The neighbors have made a _____ about people playing music too loudly at night.
    (1) complaint   (2) argument
    (3) disagreement   (4) compliment   (   )

Section E: Synonyms MCQs   (5 marks)

Read the passage. Then, choose the answer closest in meaning to the underlined word and write its number in the brackets.

Last night, a fire broke out in an empty warehouse. Four fire engines reached the scene within a few minutes and the firemen fought the (21) underlined blazing building for about an hour before bringing it under control. The final flames were all (22) extinguished by 3 o'clock this morning. At this point experts could enter the building to (23) investigate the cause of the fire. A police (24) spokesperson said that people living in the neighborhood had reported hearing an explosion shortly before the fire broke out. The warehouse had previously been used to store chemicals used in (25) fertilizers. The company which owns the warehouse denied that it had left dangerous chemicals in the building. No one was injured in the fire.

21. (1) bright   (2) burning
    (3) enormous   (4) industrial   (   )

22. (1) spread out   (2) washed out
    (3) put out   (4) taken out   (   )

23. (1) look into   (2) write up
    (3) talk about   (4) confirm   (   )

24. (1) representative   (2) guard
    (3) visitor   (4) trainee   (   )

25. (1) substances used to make soft drinks
    (2) substances used to make medicine
    (3) substances used to make animal food
    (4) substances used to make plants grow better   (   )

Section F: Comprehension MCQs (5 marks)

Read the passage and answer the questions.

George Stephenson was a British engineer who was born in 1781. His parents could not read or write, and since his father was a fireman earning only a low wage, there was not enough money to send George or his brothers and sisters to school. When George was eight he started to work on a farm. When he was 14 he went to work at a coal mine with new lifts, taking the miners down into **5** the ground and bringing up the coal that they dug out. George realized that education was important, so he used his wages to pay for night school, where he learned to read and write.

One day when the lift broke down, George was able to repair it, even though he had never had any training in fixing things. **10**

At that time mining was a very dangerous occupation. The miners used lamps with open flames and often these caused terrible explosions as gas leaked from the mine and was ignited by the lamps, causing the deaths of many miners. George was very concerned about these accidents and he invented a safety lamp that could be used in the mines and would not cause explosions. **15**

George designed his first train in 1814. It was a traveling engine that could pull 30 tons of coal up a hill. One of the problems at this time was that the trains were too heavy for the wooden rails they ran on and iron rails broke easily. George managed to improve the iron rails so that they were stronger.

As George's success grew, he was hired to build bigger railways such as the **20** one between Manchester and Liverpool. He realized that even small hills slowed down the trains, so he made sure the railway between Manchester and Liverpool was kept as level as possible. The opening ceremony of this railway was a great event involving a procession of eight trains driven by George and members of his family.

25

George was involved in the building of many other railways in Britain. Although he did not invent the train, he was a **pioneer** in mechanical engineering and paved the way for other engineers to improve railways in Britain and other countries.

George Stephenson died in 1848.

Choose the correct answer and write its number in the brackets.

26. George did not go to school because _____.
    (1) his parents could not read and write
    (2) his father was a fireman
    (3) his parents could not afford to send him there
    (4) he started work when he was eight   (   )

27. The lamp that George invented _____.
    (1) melted
    (2) was very expensive
    (3) could be used safely underground
    (4) was very dangerous   (   )

28. The iron rails that George made _____.
    (1) were too heavy
    (2) were very breakable
    (3) broke the engines
    (4) could take the weight of heavy engines   (   )

29. The railway between Manchester and Liverpool _____.
    (1) was built on small hills
    (2) was a tiny railway
    (3) was constructed on flat ground
    (4) was built by members of his family   (   )

30. The word 'pioneer' in line 27 means _____.
    (1) doctor
    (2) one of the first people
    (3) engineer
    (4) student   (   )

Section G: Grammar cloze   (10 marks)

Choose the correct word(s) from the box for each blank. Write its letter in the blank. Use each word(s) once.

A	aren't you	B	had read	C	have you	D	are you
E	had given	F	didn't you	G	had invited	H	gave
J	shall we	K	bought	L	had appeared	M	will we
N	arrived	P	invited	Q	read		

Lucy was looking forward to Saturday as her friend Katy (31) _____ her to her birthday party. On Saturday morning Lucy went shopping and (32) _____ Katy a book as a birthday present. It was the latest in the *Mixton Towers Mystery Books* series. Lucy knew that Katy (33) _____ all the other books in this adventure series, but this book (34) _____ in the shops only a week before. At 3 o'clock Lucy (35) _____ at the party and gave her gift to Katy. As Katy opened the present, Lucy watched her attentively. But Katy's face fell when she saw what the book was.

"You haven't read it already, (36) _____?" asked Lucy.

"No, I haven't read it. But Emily gave me the same book just a few minutes ago."
Just at that moment Katy's mother came into the room.

"Another present!" she said. "You are lucky, (37) _____?" But then she saw
that it was the same book that Emily (38) _____ Katy. "I expect you bought
the book at Popper's Book Shop, (39) _____?" she said to Lucy. "Don't worry.
I know the manager well. We will be able to change it for another book. Now let's all
sit down and have some birthday cake, (40) _____?"

Section H: Editing   (10 marks)

**The words in bold have spelling errors and the underlined words are
grammatical errors. Write the correct word in the box.**

All schools, companies and public buildings must have fire regulations clearly

(41) [   ]   (42) [   ]

displayed. It is the **responsability** of everyone who <u>enter</u> a building to familiarize

(43) [   ]

himself or herself with <u>this</u> regulations and the procedure to follow in case of a fire.

(44) [   ]

Emergency exits must be <u>indicating</u>. The electricity used to power these indicators

(45) [   ]

must come from a **seperate** generator and function even during power cuts. Fire

practice drills must be held at least once a year. The occupants of the building must

(46) [   ]

must assemble at a **dezignated** area and wait there for instructions. A roll call must

103

be taken to ensure that everyone <u>have</u> left the building. The time taken to **evackuate**

(49)

the building should be noted and should never **exeed** 15 minutes. The fire brigade

(50)

will visit schools and companies to explain the <u>important</u> of these regulations.

Section I: Comprehension cloze   (15 marks)

Read and fill in each blank with the best word.

My cousin is taking a gap year before he continues (51) _____

studies next year. He is 18 and will finish school in July. He has applied

(52) _____ go to college, but has postponed the start for another year.

Meanwhile, in his gap year he is (53) _____ to get a job for three

months to earn enough (54) _____ to go to India for the rest of the year.

He has (55) _____ offered a job in a restaurant near where he lives.

Working (56) _____ a waiter, he will earn enough to buy his plane

(57) _____. After the three months are over, he will fly to New Delhi

(58) _____ he will spend a few days seeing the sights. Then he will travel

(59) _____ train to a small town about 200 km north of the capital.

He has a job volunteering in (60) _____ school there. He will be a class

assistant. He has no teaching qualifications (61) _____ experience, but

he is very motivated and willing to (62) _____ the teachers in any way

he can. I'm sure the children will benefit (63) _____ having my cousin in

their school, and at the (64) _____ time my cousin will learn a lot about

children and about (65) _____.

104

Section J: Combining sentences

Rewrite the sentence(s) using the words(s) given. Your answer must be in one sentence and its meaning must be the same as that of the given sentence(s).

66. It was very cold today. The water in the lake froze.

_____ so _____ that

_____

67. The President opened this university ten years ago.

This university _____

_____

68. Ken came to the picnic. Ken wasn't invited to the picnic.

_____ even though

_____

69. If you don't hurry, you will miss the bus.

Unless _____

_____

70. It was a surprise for me to be picked for the team.

I was _____

_____

105

Section K: Comprehension questions   (20 marks)

Read the passage and answer the questions. Write your answers in complete sentences.

Opera is a form of music and drama. One could describe it as a sung play, but it is more than that as it also includes passages of spoken text. It has acting, scenery and costumes and is always accompanied by music. Usually a live orchestra plays in the opera house.

Opera has been described as the most glamorous and expensive art form.   **5**
It has produced some of the most powerful music ever written. It is expensive as it demands impressive sets, often has a large cast who must be dressed in grand costumes, an orchestra and a venue.

The first operas were composed in the 16th century in Italy and these are still performed today. Opera spread in popularity across Europe and each nation   **10**
developed its own tradition of opera. But Italy continued to be the best and many operas performed today all over the world are sung in Italian. Many opera houses now provide a translation of the words being sung into the language of the country it is performed in. Words are shown on a board above the stage to enable the audience to follow the performance, even if they do not understand   **15**
the language of the opera.

Many famous operas are based on plays or stories. *The Marriage of Figaro* is an opera that was composed by Mozart. It is based on a play of the same name written by French playwright Beaumarchais.

Carmen is another famous opera, composed by the French musician Bizet, and   **20**
based on a short story by Prosper Merimée. It is about a Spanish gypsy girl

Carmen, who works in a cigarette factory. She falls in love with a soldier.
A story of jealousy, madness and murder unfolds with a tragic ending. This opera
is perhaps the most famous in the world, with many of the arias, or songs, being
very well-known.   **25**

Over the years opera has changed from being a popular form of entertainment
for many of the middle classes, to an exclusive art form for the wealthy.
These days it is still seen by some as snobbish and expensive, whereas others
appreciate it and value it highly. Although the best seats for an opera are
expensive, most opera companies ensure that affordable tickets are available for   **30**
students and those on smaller incomes. In this way performances can be enjoyed
by all. Recordings of all of the major operas sung by the most famous singers
are now available on both CDs and DVDs. People who cannot attend a live
performance can still get to know and enjoy opera through these recordings.

71. Why is it inaccurate to describe opera as a 'sung play'?

_____

_____

72. Why is opera expensive?

_____

_____

_____

73. If opera is performed in a language that the audience do not understand,
    how do the audience follow what happens in the performance?

_____

_____

_____

74. What did Beaumarchais do?

_____

_____

75. Where does the story of *Carmen* come from?

_____

_____

76. Who was Carmen?

_____

_____

77. Which word in paragraph 5 means 'song'?

_____

_____

78. What kind of people originally went to the opera?

_____

_____

79. What do people think of opera today?

_____

_____

_____

80. How can you discover opera if you cannot go to a live performance?

_____

_____

Date: _____

Practice Paper 8

Section A: Comprehension MCQs
(5 marks)

Read the notice and answer the questions.

Come to the Greenery Garden Center for all your outdoor needs.

A whole range of seasonal garden plants are kept in stock for your flowerbeds and your vegetable patch.

An exciting choice of indoor plants are also on sale all year round.

For the whole family to enjoy the garden why not treat yourself to some top-of-the-range garden furniture?

And don't forget garden fun! Swings of the highest safety standards to suit every garden size. Paddling pools for our youngest customers and inflatable swimming pools are also available.

Are you a keen gardener? Check out our latest garden tools and machinery to make even the most difficult garden chore a pleasant task.

Beautify your garden with sculptures and water features.

While you browse in our greenhouse and visit outdoor displays, your children can enjoy our supervised play area. A protected playground offers children a safe environment to enjoy themselves while parents take their time to shop.

Try out our Organic Café for tasty nutritious snacks. The café is open daily from 11 a.m. till 6 p.m.

The center is open every day, weekdays from 9 a.m. till 7 p.m., Saturdays from 8.30 a.m. till 8.30 p.m. and Sundays from 10 a.m till 6 p.m.

Choose the correct answer and write its number in the brackets.

1. What type of plants can you buy at the Greenery Garden Center?
   (1) every type of plant
   (2) flowers and vegetables in season and house plants
   (3) house plants
   (4) all types of flowers and vegetables   (   )

2. The machinery on sale _____.
   (1) is for supervised use only
   (2) is on display in the greenhouse
   (3) makes boring work fun
   (4) can be used in the playground   (   )

3. While the adults shop, children can _____.
   (1) play in the paddling pool
   (2) swim in the inflatable pool
   (3) play in the playground
   (4) be supervised in the greenhouse   (   )

4. Sculptures and water features are used to _____.
   (1) water the plants
   (2) entertain the children
   (3) make your garden more attractive
   (4) make your garden work easier   (   )

5. If you go to the Greenery Garden Center when it opens on Sunday morning, you will have to wait _____ for the café to open.
   (1) 1 hour
   (2) 2 hours
   (3) 2.5 hours
   (4) 3 hours   (   )

Section B: Grammar MCQs   (7 marks)

Choose the correct answer and write its number in the brackets.

6. Remember _____ your swimming things tomorrow.
    (1) bringing   (2) bring
    (3) brought   (4) to bring   (   )

7. You _____ wait for me, but you can if you want to.
    (1) must   (2) shouldn't
    (3) don't have to   (4) mustn't   (   )

8. Be careful _____ traffic when you cross the road.
    (1) on   (2) at
    (3) off   (4) of   (   )

9. The river Nile is one of _____ rivers in the world.
    (1) the longest   (2) longer
    (3) longest   (4) long   (   )

10. The History Museum _____ by the president six months ago.
    (1) opened   (2) is opened
    (3) was opening   (4) was opened   (   )

11. Jenny _____ to school every day now.
    (1) walks   (2) is walking
    (3) was walking   (4) walked   (   )

12. _____ of the very hot weather, the flowers in the garden died.
    (1) Although   (2) Despite
    (3) Even though   (4) As a result   (   )

Section C: Punctuation MCQs (3 marks)

Read the passage. Then, choose the correct answer and write its number in the brackets.

Ice hockey is a team game played on ice. In Canada and the US it is referred to simply as 'hockey' (13) ◯ It is a game popular in countries which are cold enough to have natural ice (14) ◯ though these days it is played in indoor ice rinks all year round. It is represented by the various national leagues, mostly for male players but women also play. The National Women (15) ◯ s Hockey League, in the US, is the highest level of ice hockey for women in the world. It is a very fast, physical game which is adapted from the game of field hockey.

13. (1) [.] full stop
    (2) [,] comma
    (3) [?] question mark
    (4) ["] quotation marks   (   )

14. (1) [.] full stop
    (2) [,] comma
    (3) [?] question mark
    (4) ["] quotation marks   (   )

15. (1) [!] exclamation mark
    (2) [,] comma
    (3) [?] question mark
    (4) ['] apostrophe   (   )

Section D: Vocabulary MCQs (5 marks)

Choose the best answer and write its number in the brackets.

16. My aunt always says she would like just a _____ of milk in her tea.
    (1) cloud   (2) blob
    (3) flood   (4) drop   (   )

17. The sunlight _____ on the water like thousands of little lights.
    (1) glowed   (2) dimmed
    (3) bounced   (4) sparkled   (   )

18. The painter decided to put three _____ of paint on the walls.
    (1) coats   (2) covers
    (3) stages   (4) dollops   (   )

19. The cat _____ up into a ball and went to sleep.
    (1) stretched   (2) straightened
    (3) curled   (4) rounded   (   )

20. Everyone _____ to Mr Ariel, our principal.
    (1) looks up   (2) looks down
    (3) looks across   (4) looks through   (   )

Section E: Synonyms MCQs (5 marks)

Read the passage. Then, choose the answer closest in meaning to the underlined word(s) and write its number in the brackets.

A pictogram is a symbol which (21) <u>stands for</u> something by drawing it. It can be a

place, an activity, a (22) <u>concept</u> or thing. Pictograms are used commonly today

to give information or instructions. In public places pictograms can (23) <u>indicate</u>

emergency exits, bus stops and train stations. Although there are many

(24) <u>universally</u>-recognized symbols, some vary from culture to culture. In some

countries, to tell apart men and women, women are drawn wearing a western-style dress, but in other cultures this can cause confusion as men also wear dress-like clothing. Although you may think that pictograms are simple to draw, it is in fact quite (25) <u>difficult</u> to clearly and simply portray an activity in such a way that it is quickly and easily recognized by many people.

21. (1) gets up   (2) represents
    (3) remain stationary   (4) waits for   (   )

22. (1) item   (2) person
    (3) idea   (4) position   (   )

23. (1) show   (2) transfer
    (3) mean   (4) open   (   )

24. (1) space   (2) galaxy
    (3) worldwide   (4) home   (   )

25. (1) straightforward   (2) impossible
    (3) easy   (4) tough   (   )

Section F: Comprehension MCQs   (5 marks)

Read the passage and answer the questions.

One bright sunny morning, a fisherman set off for his favorite spot on the river. His wife waved goodbye and wished him 'tight lines'. By this she meant she hoped he would catch some fish. The man walked along the riverbank until he found a place that was free from overhanging branches that could tangle his fishing line. He looked into the deep dark water for any sign of fish. He laid down   **5** his bag and attended to his fishing rod. He attached a small fly with a hook in it to the end of the line and reeled out the line. He flicked the rod back into the air and with a twist of his wrist threw the line into the water. The fly at the end of the line danced across the surface of the water.

The fisherman reeled in his line and repeated the process of throwing the fly   **10**
into the water. After a while, he walked down the river and chose another spot. Perhaps there would be fish there, he thought to himself. He flicked his line into the water.

Suddenly a fish darted up from the bottom of the river and took the fly in its mouth. The fisherman **jerked** the rod until the line was tight. He reeled it in as the fish   **15**
fought to escape. Lifting the rod up, the fisherman dangled the fish in the air and then let it land slowly on the grass. The man took the hook out of the fish's mouth, making sure the fish was not injured. He held its glistening slippery body in his two hands and kneeled on the ground over the river bank. Immersing the fish into the water, the man released it from his hands and watched it swim   **20**
gracefully away.

"Did you have any tight lines?" his wife asked him when he reached
home a few hours later.
"Yes," replied the man.
"So do we have fish for supper tonight?"   **25**
"Oh no," he replied. "I put the fish back. It seemed cruel to kill it."

Choose the correct answer and write its number in the brackets.

26. The man chose a spot without overhanging branches because _____.
    (1) there were more fish there
    (2) his line would not be caught on the branches
    (3) he could see fish there
    (4) he could put a fly on his line   (   )

27. When he threw the fly into the river _____.
    (1) it sank to the bottom
    (2) it bounced up into the air
    (3) it moved across the top of the water
    (4) he pulled it out immediately   (   )

28. The word 'jerked' in line 15 means _____.
    (1) quickly moved
    (2) gently moved
    (3) slowly moved
    (4) kept still   (   )

29. The man took the hook out of the fish's mouth _____.
    (1) harshly
    (2) hurriedly
    (3) easily
    (4) gently   (   )

30. The couple did not eat fish that night because _____.
    (1) the fisherman had let the fish go
    (2) they did not like fish
    (3) the fisherman had not caught a fish
    (4) the fisherman's wife thought fishing was cruel   (   )

Section G: Grammar cloze   (10 marks)

Choose the correct word(s) from the box for each blank. Write its letter in the blank. Use each word(s) once.

A	should	B	where	C	have to	D	could	E	who
F	when	G	don't have to	H	more	J	what	K	must
L	less	M	most	N	which	P	might	Q	shall

What I like about the school holidays is that I (31) _____ get up early. I can stay in bed as long as I like. Usually, I get up at about 8 o'clock, (32) _____ is an hour later than on a school day. There are still chores that I (33) _____ do, such as washing up the breakfast things and taking the dog for a walk, but during the holidays I have much more time to do them, so they seem (34) _____ enjoyable. I like to take the dog through the woods to the river. He has a favorite spot (35) _____ he likes to paddle in the water. After a walk, I (36) _____ play on my computer for a while, or if not, I sometimes go to the park to meet a friend. I try to use my time wisely, as my mother always tells me that I (37) _____ never waste time. But sometimes it's nice just to do nothing! The (38) _____ enjoyable days are those when we go to the beach with the whole family. We take a picnic and play games on the sand. I (39) _____ easily spend every day there. Still, all good things (40) _____ come to an end, and school holidays are no exception.

Section H: Editing   (10 marks)

The words in bold have spelling errors and the underlined words are grammatical errors. Write the correct word in the box.

(41) [   ]

There is a warning of possible floods in the Dale area of the city. Due to the <u>recently</u>

rains and with more heavy storms forecast, there is a danger that the river will flood

(42) [   ]   (43) [   ]

<u>his</u> banks. People living in the area are **adviced** to leave their houses, taking only

(44) [   ]   (45) [   ]

their most **prescios** possessions. Rescue services will be <u>on</u> operation throughout the

(46) [   ]

day and any citizens requiring help of any kind should <u>contacting</u> these services as

(47) [   ]   (48) [   ]

soon as possible. These **precautionery** measures will, it is <u>hope</u>, only be necessary

(49) [   ]

for the next 24 hours. As soon as the situation **improoves**, residents of the area

willbe allowed back into their homes. Schools in the area will be kept for

(50) [   ]

acommodating people, and so there will be no lessons for the children.

Section I: Comprehension cloze   (15 marks)

Read and fill in each blank with the best word.

The winter solstice occurs around 21st December in the northern hemisphere. It is the shortest day of the year. There are the (51) _____ number of daylight hours on this day. Traditionally, this marks the first day (52) _____ winter, though, in other traditions it is also considered (53) _____ the middle of winter.

This period of the year is celebrated (54) _____ many different cultures and in different ways. Some people celebrate by (55) _____ into their homes green branches, or trees and plants with red berries (56) _____ decorate them. This could be the origins of the Christmas tree. This time is also associated (57) _____ feasting, singing and dancing to mark a period of rebirth. In some places (58) _____ is considered important in every home to keep a fire (59) _____ throughout this night.

In the southern (60) _____, where the seasons are the opposite of the north, this date marks the longest (61) _____ of the year, or the summer solstice. This is also celebrated. In northern countries (62) _____ summer solstice occurs on 21st June. In the far north (63) _____ this day, the sun never sets completely and (64) _____ it never becomes dark during the night. In countries close to the equator the days and nights are the same length throughout the (65) _____.

Section J: Combining sentences

Rewrite the sentence(s) using the words(s) given. Your answer must be in one sentence and its meaning must be the same as that of the given sentence(s).

66. The sun was shining. The day was still cold.

Although _____

_____

67. Unless you hurry, you will be late.

If _____

_____

68. Jack practiced the trumpet every day. Jack passed his trumpet exam with top marks.

As a result _____

_____

69. "It's true I copied Matt's homework," said John.

John admitted _____

_____

70. My father grew up in a village. The village is now a big town.

_____ where _____

_____

Section K: Comprehension questions

（20 marks)

Read the passage and answer the questions. Write your answers in complete sentences.

There are some amazing stories of animals showing that they are more intelligent than we think.

I once read about a boy who was playing with some balls and a bat in his back yard. He would throw a ball against the wall of the garage and when it bounced off the wall he would hit it with a bat. Unfortunately, he wasn't very **5** accurate when he hit the ball and instead of the ball returning to the garage wall, it sometimes shot off elsewhere. Then the boy would have to run off and find the ball in the garden. At the edge of the garden stood an old pear tree, with many branches. On several occasions the boy hit a ball into the branches of the pear tree. The ball stayed in the tree. This happened so many times that eventually the **10** boy had no more balls to play with. He went to shake the tree, but nothing fell out of it, apart from a few dead leaves and an unripe pear. He threw his bat into the tree to knock the balls down, but the bat ended up stuck in the tree too!

The boy turned away thinking he would have to give up and find something else to do, when he saw the family cat which had been watching him. The cat sat still **15** for a moment then skilfully climbed up the pear tree and, one-by-one, knocked down the balls and the bat that had been stuck in the tree.

Another of my favorite stories is about a dog which got lost. Its owners had taken a train to a mountain village about 20 km from their home. They had decided to walk back down the valley, a walk of about three hours. When they got off the **20** train, they set off with their dog on its leash, their map in their hand and their picnic in their backpacks. After about an hour and a half they stopped to

121

have their picnic. They chose a spot with a magnificent view of the mountains, a wooded valley in the distance and a small stream behind them. They sat in the sun and enjoyed their lunch. They let the dog off its leash to wander around **25** freely. After about half an hour, they wanted to continue their hike, but when they called the dog, he was nowhere to be seen. They looked everywhere, they called and called, but no dog came. They asked anyone they saw, but no one had seen the dog. After waiting around and searching for three hours they decided they had to give up. Sadly, they continued down the valley to their home. **30**

When they arrived at the train station **from where** they had caught the train that morning, what should they see but their dog! How had he got there? Just as they were greeting the dog with joyous cries, a girl came up to them. She explained that she had taken the train down from the village about an hour ago. The dog had been waiting at the station and had followed her onto the train, back to his **35** home town.

71. How do some humans regard animals?

_____

_____

72. What game was the boy playing in the garden?

_____

_____

_____

73. Describe the pear tree.

_____

_____

74. Which word in paragraph 3 means 'without moving'?

_____

_____

75. What did the hikers have with them when they left the train station at the village?

_____

_____

76. Where did the hikers have their lunch?

_____

_____

_____

77. How did the hikers try to find their dog?

_____

_____

78. Why do you think the hikers were sad when they continued down the valley back to their home?

_____

_____

79. What does 'from where' in line 31 refer to?

_____

_____

80. How did the dog reach his home town?

_____

_____

_____

Answer Key

Practice Paper 1 p. 6

Comprehension MCQs

1. (3)   2. (2)   3. (3)   4. (4)   5. (3)

Grammar MCQs

6. (3)   7. (4)   8. (2)   9. (4)   10. (1)
11. (4)   12. (2)

Puntuation MCQs

13. (3)   14. (3)   15. (1)

Vocabulary MCQs

16. (3)   17. (1)   18. (4)   19. (1)   20. (2)

Synonyms MCQs

21. (4)   22. (1)   23. (2)   24. (3)   25. (2)

Comprehension MCQs

26. (3)   27. (2)   28. (4)   29. (1)   30. (1)

Grammar cloze

31. B   32. G   33. J   34. M   35. F
36. C   37. H   38. A   39. E   40. P

Editing

41. stolen
42. swimming
43. left
44. immediately
45. locked
46. distraught
47. brings/will bring
48. beautifully
49. suspicious
50. nearest

Comprehension cloze

51. be
52. been
53. are
54. when
55. enough/some
56. the
57. can
58. of
59. if
60. money
61. made/earned
62. audience/viewers
63. break
64. go
65. products

Combining sentences

66. Our living room is being painted by a decorator.
67. Caroline has lived in Brazil since 2006.
68. My mother asked (me) if I would like something to drink.
69. The tennis match was canceled because of the rain.
70. Penny was so hungry when she got home from school that she ate a whole packet of cookies.

Comprehension questions

71. A mosquito is usually not longer than 16 mm and it weighs about 2.5 g.
72. The word 'nocturnal' means something sleeps in the day and is active at night.
73. The mosquito is described as the most dangerous animal on Earth because it spreads very serious diseases which cause the deaths of 5 million people a year.
74. A mosquito sucks blood from people. If it sucks blood from someone who is infected with a disease, the next person the mosquito bites can be infected through the saliva of the mosquito.
75. Malaria and yellow fever are two diseases spread by mosquitos.
76. If the land is dry, the mosquitos cannot breed. They need water to reproduce.
77. 'This' refers to insect repellent.
78. People sleep under nets to stop the insects from biting them.
79. Vaccines provide immunity to diseases, so people do not develop the diseases.
80. *Accept any reasonable answer.*

Practice Paper 2 p. 20

Comprehension MCQs

1. (3)   2. (2)   3. (1)   4. (1)   5. (4)

Grammar MCQs

6. (4)   7. (1)   8. (2)   9. (1)   10. (4)
11. (3)   12. (2)

Punctuation MCQs

13. (2)   14. (2)   15. (1)

Vocabulary MCQs

16. (4)   17. (1)   18. (4)   19. (3)   20. (2)

Synonyms MCQs

21. (3)   22. (1)   23. (4)   24. (2)   25. (2)

Comprehension MCQs

26. (4)   27. (3)   28. (1)   29. (3)   30. (1)

Grammar cloze

31. N   32. P   33. L   34. M   35. Q
36. B   37. G   38. D   39. E   40. J

Editing

41. wasn't
42. ladder
43. was
44. waiting
45. Emergency
46. saw
47. X-ray
48. was
49. twisted
50. chore

Comprehension cloze

51. is
52. can/may/might/will/could
53. may/might
54. batteries
55. pack/deck
56. be
57. labeled/marked
58. Any

59. on   60. let
61. with   62. If
63. safe   64. will
65. be

Combining sentences

66. Despite the heavy rain, the match was still played.
67. George has been living (has lived) in London for three years.
68. The children were making so much noise (that) I didn't hear the phone ring.
69. You will be late unless you hurry up.
70. You must write the essay without using a dictionary.

Comprehension questions

71. The phrase 'behind the scenes' describes a situation which is not seen.
72. People who work at the check-in desks take our luggage and give us a boarding pass.
73. People who work on the runways make sure that the runways are clear of objects or animals.
74. Hand luggage is checked by the security staff.
75. The word 'flocks' means groups of birds.
76. Bangers are used to frighten away the birds.
77. Dogs can get under the fence which surrounds the airport or they can escape from the cage in which they were traveling.
78. The word 'they' refers to the dogs.
79. The word 'tarmac' means runway.
80. Salt causes damage to the planes.

Practice Paper 3 p. 34

Comprehension MCQs

1. (3)   2. (2)   3. (3)   4. (3)   5. (2)

Grammar MCQs

6. (3)   7. (4)   8. (3)   9. (1)   10. (4)
11. (4)   12. (4)

Punctuation MCQs

13. (4)   14. (2)   15. (3)

Vocabulary MCQs

16. (3)   17. (4)   18. (3)   19. (2)   20. (3)

Synonyms MCQs

21. (3)   22. (1)   23. (3)   24. (1)   25. (2)

Comprehension MCQs

26. (3)   27. (4)   28. (2)   29. (2)   30. (1)

Grammar cloze

31. D   32. A   33. K   34. B   35. F
36. G   37. P   38. N   39. L   40. M

Editing

41. despite   42. to grow
43. deep   44. shallow
45. quickly   46. absorbed
47. which/that   48. fleshy

49. store   50. enables

Comprehension cloze

51. company/companionship   52. very
53. old   54. committing
55. down   56. When/Before
57. by/with   58. have
59. everyone   60. fond
61. who   62. be
63. had   64. When/After
65. home/place

Combining sentences

66. If I weren't so short, I would play basketball.
67. It was the first time Eric had ever seen so much snow.
68. In spite of the heavy rain, the team won the match.
69. All this work must be/has to be finished by tomorrow.
70. Steve regretted resigning from his job.

Comprehension questions

71. The word 'relaxing' means resting.
72. It was in the evening.
73. He was tired, he had had a tiring week, and he was looking forward to a relaxing weekend.
74. The word 'hovering' means staying in one place in the air.
75. The word 'it' refers to the light.
76. Bob had left home at 6 p.m.
77. After the car stopped Bob was surrounded by the light.
78. Bob didn't remember anything about what happened.
79. Bob thought that Anne would ask a lot of questions that he would not be able to answer.
80. *Accept any reasonable answer.*

Practice Paper 4 p. 48

Comprehension MCQs

1. (4)   2. (3)   3. (3)   4. (4)   5. (2)

Grammar MCQs

6. (3)   7. (4)   8. (2)   9. (4)   10. (2)
11. (3)   12. (3)

Punctuation MCQs

13. (4)   14. (1)   15. (1)

Vocabulary MCQs

16. (3)   17. (2)   18. (4)   19. (1)   20. (4)

Synonyms MCQs

21. (2)   22. (1)   23. (3)   24. (2)   25. (1)

Comprehension MCQs

26. (1)   27. (2)   28. (2)   29. (3)   30. (4)

Grammar cloze

31. D   32. G   33. P   34. M   35. L
36. E   37. C   38. N   39. Q   40. B

Editing

41. who   42. does
43. is   44. restrictions

45. contract   46. doing
47. ride   48. careers
49. to have   50. insist

Comprehension cloze

51. as   52. been
53. in
54. put/launched/sent   55. between
56. own   57. For
58. experiments/purposes/research
59. to   60. weather
61. also   62. important/numerous/common
63. satellites   64. longer
65. that

Combining sentences

66. That's the funniest story I have ever heard.
67. Jeff wishes he were rich.
68. Kate has lived in Germany for 5 years.
69. The teacher told the children not to make so much noise.
70. Emily went shopping while her sister was tidying their bedroom.

Comprehension questions

71. The word 'livestock' means animals that are kept on a farm.
72. The *Forfarshire* was going to Dundee.
73. The *Forfarshire* broke up because it hit a rock.
74. A lifeboat didn't go to rescue the survivors because the sea was too rough.
75. The nine people waiting to be rescued were terrified and exhausted.
76. Grace and her father couldn't take all nine people at once because their boat could only hold five of them.
77. After the rescue, Grace was given many medals for her bravery.
78. Grace didn't appear on stage because she was a very humble person.
79. 'Tuberculosis' is a disease for which there was no cure at the time that Grace was alive.
80. The word 'which' refers to the disease tuberculosis.

Practice Paper 5 p. 62

Comprehension MCQs

1. (4)   2. (2)   3. (4)   4. (2)   5. (4)

Grammar MCQs

6. (1)   7. (3)   8. (4)   9. (4)   10. (3)
11. (4) 12. (2)

Punctuation MCQs

13. (2) 14. (1) 15. (4)

Vocabulary MCQs

16. (3) 17. (4) 18. (3) 19. (4) 20. (2)

Synonyms MCQs

21. (2) 22. (1) 23. (3) 24. (3) 25. (2)

Comprehension MCQs

26. (3) 27. (2) 28. (2) 29. (2) 30. (4)

Grammar cloze

31. H   32. L   33. P   34. K   35. G
36. E   37. D   38. A   39. N   40. M

Editing

41. showing   42. which/that
43. magnetic   44. so/thus
45. navigate   46. rubbing
47. piece   48. float
49. known   50. do

Comprehension cloze

51. from   52. escalators/them
53. can   54. during/for
55. occur/work   56. down
57. There   58. you
59. other   60. for
61. which   62. the
63. and   64. either
65. on

Combining sentences

66. Although Jack felt unwell, he sat for his final exam.
67. It was the most beautiful dress Kate had ever seen.
68. The road was built by the Romans almost 2,000 years ago./The road was built almost 2,000 years ago by the Romans.
69. There will be a slight rise in the temperature tomorrow.
70. Unless you try hard, you won't be picked for the team.

Comprehension questions

71. Parents tell their children nursery rhymes to entertain them, calm them down and to teach them words and numbers.
72. The word 'fleece' means the wool coat of a lamb.
73. Mary Sawyer was a little girl who lived on a farm. She had a pet lamb.
74. Everyone at school was very excited to see the lamb.
75. John Roulston wrote the first few verses of the poem, but it is not known if he wrote the remaining verses or if Sarah Hale did.
76. Approximately 100,000 people died in England from the plague.
77. People thought that the plague was spread by bad smells. They thought that if you carried something nice-smelling, like flowers, in your pocket, you would be protected from the plague.
78. Humpty Dumpty sat on a wall and then fell off it. He was broken into pieces when he fell off.
79. The word 'them' refers to nursery rhymes.
80. Some nursery rhymes have been lost because they were never written down.

Practice Paper 6 p. 78

Comprehension MCQs

1. (3)   2. (3)   3. (4)   4. (2)   5. (4)

Grammar MCQs

6. (3) 7. (1) 8. (3) 9. (4) 10. (4)
11. (2) 12. (3)

Punctuation MCQs

13. (4) 14. (4) 15. (4)

Vocabulary MCQs

16. (3) 17. (4) 18. (2) 19. (4) 20. (1)

Synonyms MCQs

21. (3) 22. (1) 23. (2) 24. (3) 25. (4)

Comprehension MCQs

26. (4) 27. (2) 28. (1) 29. (3) 30. (2)

Grammar cloze

31. P 32. A 33. K 34. B 35. F
36. E 37. H 38. L 39. C 40. J

Editing

41. sewn 42. worn
43. saying 44. enough
45. buy 46. occasion
47. was 48. sleeves
49. buy 50. assistant

Comprehension cloze

51. an 52. there
53. with/to 54. have
55. babies/mammals/animals
56. lot 57. crops/fields
58. growing 59. ways/means/methods
60. discovered/found 61. their
62. run/hop 63. away
64. is 65. away

Combining sentences

66. Paul said we wouldn't go for a walk, unless it stopped raining.
67. I was amazed by the display of flowers in the reception area.
68. It's worth visiting the new exhibition at the museum.
69. Jenny washed up the dishes so that her mother could have a rest.
70. You can't use the photocopier because it is being repaired.

Comprehension questions

71. Sam didn't finish his homework properly because he was fed up with doing it. He wanted to go outside.
72. Sam felt that he deserved some time to enjoy himself.
73. Sam left the house rudely. He raced off on his bike.
74. Sam cycled onto a track that led into the woods.
75. Sam got off his bike and saw the puncture because his bike became very hard to ride.
76. Sam hadn't taken a repair kit with him because he had left the house in a temper. He had left very quickly.
77. There were so many bike tracks in the dirt he didn't know which ones were from his bike.
78. Sam sat down in the clearing because he was tired, lost and didn't know where to go.

79. Sam wished he hadn't left the house in such a hurry and bad temper and he wished he had told someone where he was going.
80. Maybe Sam thought he didn't deserve any help because he had refused to help his parents when they asked him for some help./Maybe Sam thought that the puncture was his own fault, so he should repair it./Maybe the puncture was Sam's punishment for being rude.

Practice Paper 7 p. 94

Comprehension MCQs

1. (2) 2. (2) 3. (1) 4. (1) 5. (2)

Grammar MCQs

6. (2) 7. (2) 8. (4) 9. (3) 10. (1)
11. (3) 12. (4)

Punctuation MCQs

13. (4) 14. (1) 15. (1)

Vocabulary MCQs

16. (3) 17. (4) 18. (1) 19. (2) 20. (1)

Synonyms MCQs

21. (2) 22. (3) 23. (1) 24. (1) 25. (4)

Comprehension MCQs

26. (3) 27. (3) 28. (4) 29. (3) 30. (2)

Grammar cloze

31. G 32. K 33. B 34. L 35. N
36. C 37. A 38. E 39. F 40. J

Editing

41. responsibility 42. enters
43. these 44. indicated
45. separate 46. designated
47. has 48. evacuate
49. exceed 50. importance

Comprehension cloze

51. his 52. to
53. going 54. money
55. been 56. as
57. ticket/fare 58. where
59. by 60. a
61. or 62. help/assist
63. from 64. same
65. India

Combining sentences

66. It was so cold today that the water in the lake froze.
67. This university was opened by the President ten years ago.
68. Ken came to the picnic even though he wasn't invited (to it).
69. Unless you hurry, you will miss the bus.
70. I was surprised to be picked for the team.

Comprehension questions

71. It is inaccurate to describe opera as a 'sung play' because it also includes passages that are spoken.

72. Opera is expensive as it needs impressive sets, often has a large cast who must be clothed in grand costumes, an orchestra and a venue.
73. If an opera is performed in a language that the audience does not understand there is a translation of the words sung. This translation is displayed above the stage.
74. Beaumarchais wrote a play called *The Marriage of Figaro*.
75. The story of *Carmen* comes from a short story written by Prosper Merimée.
76. Carmen was a Spanish gypsy girl who worked in a cigarette factory.
77. The word 'aria' means song.
78. Originally many of the middle classes went to the opera.
79. These days some people think opera is snobbish and expensive. Other people appreciate it and value it highly.
80. If you cannot go to a live performance of an opera, you can listen to recordings on CD or DVD.

Practice Paper 8 p. 109

Comprehension MCQs
1. (2) 2. (3) 3. (3) 4. (3) 5. (1)

Grammar MCQs
6. (4) 7. (3) 8. (4) 9. (1) 10. (4)
11. (1) 12. (4)

Punctuation MCQs
13. (1) 14. (2) 15. (4)

Vocabulary MCQs
16. (4) 17. (4) 18. (1) 19. (3) 20. (1)

Synonyms MCQs
21. (2) 22. (3) 23. (1) 24. (3) 25. (4)

Comprehension MCQs
26. (2) 27. (3) 28. (1) 29. (4) 30. (1)

Grammar cloze
31. G 32. N 33. C 34. H 35. B
36. P 37. A 38. M 39. D 40. K

Editing
41. recent
42. its
43. advised
44. precious
45. in
46. contact
47. precautionary
48. hoped
49. improves
50. accommodating

Comprehension cloze
51. fewest/least
52. of
53. as
54. by
55. bringing
56. to
57. with
58. it
59. burning/going
60. hemisphere
61. day
62. the
63. on
64. so
65. year

Combining sentences
66. Although the sun was shining, the day was still cold.
67. If you don't hurry, you will be late.
68. As a result of practicing the trumpet every day, Jack passed his trumpet exam with top marks.
69. John admitted copying Matt's homework.
70. The village where my father grew up is now a big town.

Comprehension questions
71. Some humans think animals are not so intelligent.
72. The boy was playing with a bat and some balls. He threw the ball against a wall and then, when it bounced back, he hit it with the bat.
73. The pear tree was old with many branches.
74. The word 'still' means without moving.
75. When the hikers left the train station they had their dog, a map and their backpacks with them.
76. The hikers had their lunch at a spot with a view of the mountains and a wooded valley. There was a stream behind them.
77. They called the dog and looked everywhere for three hours. They asked everyone they saw if they had seen the dog.
78. They were probably sad because they had lost their dog.
79. The phrase 'from where' refers to the train station in their home town.
80. When the dog got lost he returned to the train station. He then followed a girl onto a train back down to his home town.